NOT
CHANGE
Brian.H.Edwards

EVANGELICAL PRESS

EVANGELICAL PRESS
16/18 High Street, Welwyn, Hertfordshire, AL6 9EQ, England

© Evangelical Press 1982

First published 1982
Second impression 1984

ISBN 0 85234 170 9

Bible quotations are from the New International Version.

Typeset in Great Britain by Cleer Typesetters, Hertford.
Printed by Ancor Brendon Ltd., Tiptree, Essex, England.

To Paul and Avril Bassett

The author would like to thank sincerely all who co-operated in the writing of this book, particularly those who made valuable criticisms of the draft and others who became part of the book by allowing their story to be retold.

Contents

		page
1.	Where it hurts most	11
2.	Back to the starting-line	31
3.	Isn't God a bit hard?	47
4.	Sense out of suffering	62
5.	Offering alternatives	81
6.	Why doesn't God do something?	105

1.
Where it hurts most

I thought we had finished, and I was about to get up and leave the surgery when the doctor detained me. 'If I may,' he enquired, 'I would like to ask you a theological question.' He went on to describe himself as a 'backsliding Presbyterian'. He had been brought up in a strongly religious environment, went to the war and came home doubting how God could allow such atrocities. 'How can you believe in a God who allows all the suffering in the world today?' This was his problem and after qualifying and practising for many years he was still asking that question. He had been trying to be 'objective' about the subject but no one had given him a satisfactory answer. In five minutes of surgery time I had to better the rest. Inevitably, I failed. In the end I had to be content with issuing a challenge: 'You may not find my explanation satisfactory, but at least with a belief in God I do have an answer to give; with no belief in God you face the same problem without any answer.' The doctor conceded the truth of that, and with this sole point of agreement we parted.

More than any other single question this is the one I am asked most often today. It comes from classroom and lecture hall, from shop-floor and boardroom, from laboratory and surgery. The question cuts right across education, nationality and religion, and generally it is

framed something like this: 'How can you believe in a God of love with all the misery and suffering in today's world? If he cares about people why doesn't he do something about it?'

Now, whichever way you look at it, that is a fair question to ask, and if the Christian hasn't a reasonable answer to give, then his faith is not worth very much. I want to try and give a Christian answer, but perhaps I ought to make it clear right from the start that this is not a comprehensive study of the subject of suffering, neither is it a theological or philosophical exposition. I want to be practical and down to earth. I want to face up to the issues we all face and simply explain how I view them as a Christian. I want to write from my personal experience, my constant contact with people, my firm Christian convictions and simply because I live in the same world of suffering as everyone else. I want to give some pointers, not a careful exposition. If you feel some arguments need further reasoning, you are probably right. I have deliberately kept the book brief in the hope that you will read it all. I am only too well aware of the temptation to 'skim', and I also know how easy it is to give up a book half-way through! My arguments are only signposts to put you on a more hopeful course than one of despair. I am not going to duck any issues or pull any punches. You may not like all my conclusions, but I want to encourage you to stay tuned right to the end of the book. Don't switch off as soon as you take exception to something I say. Who knows? You may find yourself in agreement by the end of the programme!

Let's make a start right at the centre of our problem.

Disasters!

A young friend of mine, who was suffering from severe depression, was advised by a colleague at work to stop reading the daily newspaper. I do not believe any of his doctors or psychiatrists offered that suggestion, but it was one of the most practical pieces of advice anyone gave him! It does not matter when you read this chapter, the news headlines will not be particularly cheerful today. Somewhere an airliner has downed, a train has crashed, a hurricane is on the rampage, a civil war has broken out or there is a heart-shattering story of personal tragedy from disease, death or violence. So often the Christian will enter his lecture hall, office or workshop later in the day to be met with a barrage of 'Why?' or 'Where is your God?' Let's put disasters into perspective. It is all too easy to assume that we have the right to ignore God for most of the time and still expect him to come running along just before we are about to make a big mistake. As a Christian I am not a fatalist. I neither shrug my shoulders helplessly and mutter, 'Whatever will be, will be', nor do I dismiss the issue with a pious 'God wills it'. Both these statements may be true, but they do not say enough for the Christian. Everything in life has a purpose, and although we may not always find it, the Christian has a duty to keep an open eye for the lessons God is teaching. The trite dismissal by Bernard Shaw that 'The only thing history teaches us is that history has nothing to teach us,' is not true for the Christian. So, let's face some issues of history and see how the Christian responds. I want to divide disasters into two categories: those that are acts of men and those for which the insurance companies off-load blame by referring to them as 'acts of God'.

Man-made disasters

At 9.15 a.m., just after the children had settled into their first lesson on the morning of 21 October 1966, a waste tip from a South Wales colliery slid into the quiet mining community of Aberfan. Of all the heart-rending tragedies of that day none was worse than the fate of the village Junior School. The black slime slithered down the man-made hillside and oozed its way into the classrooms. Unable to escape, five teachers and 109 children died. The deputy head was teaching his class of thirty-four nine and ten year olds when the tip hit the school; he threw himself over the nearest three children and pushed a blackboard across another two. That was how rescue workers found them. The entire class and their teacher were engulfed under many feet of suffocating mud. The town and the nation were numb with grief. I visited Aberfan some time later and walked passed the school. Black mud, now set hard, spilled out of the classroom windows. An awful stillness of death and sorrow hung almost audibly over the town. I felt sick at the thought of that terrible day when 116 village children and twenty-eight adults died.

I remember a clergyman being interviewed by a B.B.C. reporter at the time of Aberfan. Fortunately I cannot recall his name, but what I do remember was his reply to the inevitable question about God. 'Well,' said the clergyman, 'I suppose we have to admit that this is one of those occasions when the Almighty made a mistake.' His reply was worse than the tragedy itself. I turned to my wife and said, 'That man does not worship the same God as I do.' If we have to abandon God in the face of a disaster of the magnitude of an Aberfan, then what kind of God is that? I would rather put my faith in the National Coal

Board or Merthyr Tydfil Council, who at least cleared up the mess afterwards.

There are thousands of alternative tragedies that I could have used here, but Aberfan seems the best because it is one of the worst. It all seemed so horrifyingly senseless, so tragically wasteful of life and human emotions. So how does the Christian begin to give an answer?

There are, of course, many plus factors to be found even in man-made tragedies, and the Christian's task is to find them. At such a time the very best in human nature is brought out. The national response to the Aberfan appeal was overwhelming. At times of tragedy, love and compassion are forthcoming often from the hardest people and a brief glimpse of how communities and neighbours should always live together breaks through the weary round of neighbourhood bickering and gossip. Those involved often learn for the first time to appreciate each other and experience values of life they have neglected or taken for granted. Our attention is inevitably drawn to those whose mind and life are shattered by a disaster, but the popular press rarely troubles to look for those who find faith, strength, courage and a deeper appreciation of life itself in the very place of tears and grief. Unfortunately, and Aberfan was no exception to this, human nature soon reasserts itself to spoil the good that can come out of tragedy. Writing to Christians suffering great persecution for their faith (another man-made tragedy), the apostle in the New Testament reminds them: 'No discipline seems pleasant at the time, but painful. Later on, however, it produces a harvest of righteousness and peace for those who have been trained by it' (Hebrews 12:11). The fact that some people are

hardened and embittered by grief no more disproves the value of such tragedies than the existence of juvenile offenders disproves the value of discipline at home and at school.

But, having said all this, I am sure there is another, and more important lesson that we are intended to learn from disasters like Aberfan. The subsequent enquiry criticized those responsible for building a slag tip over a small stream and so close to a school. There had been previous slips as this man-made mountain of waste grew to its final height of over one hundred feet and, though without loss of life, they ought to have served as a warning to discontinue tipping at this point. In other words, the whole tragedy was the result of human error. 'I defy any coroner to call this an act of God,' declared a Presbyterian minister at Aberfan the Sunday following the tragedy. 'That tip should never have been there. It was far too near the school.' In more restrained language the official tribunal of enquiry came to the same conclusion: 'Our strong and unanimous view is that the Aberfan disaster could and should have been prevented.' But even the tribunal allowed itself the liberty of such a description as 'bungling ineptitude'! I know this is no comfort to parents in agony, but we are not at the moment counselling parents, we are finding reasons. Truth must sometimes be coldly dispassionate. The clergyman who paraded his unbelief to the B.B.C. would have been wiser to hold his counsel until after the official enquiry. As a matter of fact, it was one of those occasions when the Coal Board made a mistake and, being wiser than the clergyman, (perhaps even having a more rational theology!) they accepted the blame.

We cannot choose as a nation to live without reference

to God and then blame him when he stands back and lets us do just that. The great lesson of Aberfan is the fallibility of man. Man is not as clever as he often tries to convince himself. This is the lesson that shouts loudly in all man-made disasters. Man is not infallible; he is not all-powerful; he is capable of foolish errors, often with serious consequences. In short, man is not God.

'We know all this,' you may respond, 'why an Aberfan to prove it?' The sad fact is that what we know and how we live are two different things. Most people, when pushed to a decision, will admit to a belief in God. But you can think like a believer and yet live like an atheist. Millions do. Man *does* live as though he can manage his affairs well enough without God. Sadly it has to be said that this was the case in the little Welsh mining town; few attended the churches and chapels, but many were ready to put God on trial for man's errors. Aberfan puts man in his place. The positive Christian note here is that when such a disaster makes man see his foolishness, ignorance and weakness, it points him at the same time to a sovereign and powerful God who, unlike man, does not make mistakes. For the man without faith in a personal God such a disaster may have no higher value than reminding the Coal Board to be more careful in future where it grows its waste tips.

There is a story in the Old Testament that illustrates this well. God instructed the Israelites to go into Canaan and take possession of the land. He told them he had planned it all, would go ahead of them and would guarantee success. The people sized up the enemy and decided it just was not on; they could not do it. They would go back to slavery in Egypt. God said, 'All right, you're on your own, if you want it that way.' At that point the men decided after all that they might as well do

something about getting into Canaan, so they sent an
expeditionary force into enemy territory. God warned
them that the timing was all wrong now and that they
would meet with no success. However, the Israelites knew
better than God and off they went to war. In a few days
they were running back into base camp as if chased by a
swarm of bees, and a host of soldiers lay dead on the field.
You can read the story in Numbers chapter 14 and
Deuteronomy chapter 1. If men leave God out of their
lives things are bound to go wrong.

In 1952, Jorge Luis Borges in *Other Inquisitions* made
this profound comment: 'There is no point in being
overwhelmed by the appalling total of human suffering;
such a total does not exist. Neither poverty nor pain is
accumulable.' Many will draw back from this and dispute
Borges's conclusion, but the value of his statement lies in
the attention he draws to the fact that a tragedy is not
worse simply because a lot of people suffer it; every
tragedy is tragedy. When a young husband and wife learn
that their toddler has been sucked under the wheels of a
juggernaut, here is another Aberfan. The same questions
arise, the same emotions are stirred. It is really no less a
tragedy. In the real terms of suffering Aberfan was not
one great disaster, but many, many individual families in
the agony of grief. We do not have to explain to a family
why someone else's child died, but why *their* child died. In
the midst of all our efforts to bring comfort and relief to
the breaking heart of a sobbing mother, there is one fact
that we just cannot avoid: when we are born into this
world we are bound up with all the experiences common
to man. Whether or not we believe in God, we gladly
accept those human experiences that are God's unique
gift to man, like family love and happiness, laughter,

peace, good food, sunshine and beauty; we can all see the value in these things. But we have to accept also the other side of human experience, like pain, disease and death, and it is not so easy to see the value in these. But strangely, there is a value. I do not expect parents, with a shattered life and aching heart, to understand everything at once. But their tragedy is not just a personal thing; we all feel it and must all learn from it. *They* may not appreciate a lesson in man's foolishness without God, but *we* who are a little more distant from the event have no excuse for failing to observe the obvious.

It is neither a mistake nor cruelty on God's part to allow such tragedies to happen. If God simply rushed to correct man's mistakes just before they produced tragic results, man would be even more convinced that he himself is infallible and can live perfectly well without God. This would make him more godless and consequently less moral and less careful in the way he lives. 'It doesn't matter how a man lives,' so we would reason, 'he gets away with it and nothing very terrible happens.' It is a 'Catch-22' situation, isn't it? Whether God allows tragedies or stops them, we would make sure he is in the wrong. If man's life was one long day of sunshine without tears you can be certain that God would not receive credit for it. But if God gets the blame for all the misery, pain and violence in the world, to whom will we give the credits for all the joy, health and beauty around us? Man must learn that he is responsible for his use of the world in which he lives. A Coal Board that tips its rubbish just anywhere, an industry that discharges its toxic waste liberally into the rivers and atmosphere, a man who drives his car after drinking heavily and the young expectant mother who insists on smoking fifty a

day must all expect tragic consequences, and the only way
people will ever learn anything is for God to stand back
and let man get on with it. Dr F. B. Meyer once said,
'Physical suffering is a smaller calamity than moral
delinquency,' and he was absolutely right. In a similar
context Paul speaks of God giving men over to their own
sinful desires (Romans 1:24).

It may all sound hard; in fact it *is* hard, but what is the
alternative if God is trying to teach us lessons we just
refuse to learn? But it is not even quite true to say that
God 'stands back' and does nothing. He has given
instructions in the Bible that, if we obeyed them, would
avoid most of man's disasters. According to the official
enquiry, the Aberfan tragedy was due to a careless
disregard of safety procedures, a callous indifference to
the lives of others and a greedy unwillingness to cut
profits by spending money to move the tip. And the Bible
has something very positive to say about each of these
reasons. If man will not obey the Maker's instructions,
whom do you blame when the machinery goes wrong?

If God *had* intervened at Aberfan, what should he have
done? Should he have diverted the underground stream?
Or perhaps performed a miracle to keep the tip at a safe
height, however much waste the Coal Board dumped on
it? Perhaps he could have arranged for it to fall on a
Saturday or stopped it two feet from the classroom
window! If it had happened that way, would all those who
in the event blamed God be believing in him now? There
are thousands of stories about 'near-misses', but few of
them stop the mad career of the world. When God does
intervene most people say, 'Whew! That was a bit of
luck!' and then get on with the dying art of living. In fact,
God had been sending out warnings for a long time: a

number of minor 'slips' at the tip had heralded the great tragedy of Aberfan, but no one took any notice. When God does intervene, who cares?

Too often in man-made disasters we react quite irrationally. One man from London sent his gift to the Aberfan disaster fund with a covering letter. It began with the hope that 'These stupid people who are to blame for this tragic disaster will be brought to justice' and closed with a P.S.: 'Don't mention God to me, there isn't one.' I wonder why he bothered with the postscript. It sounds as though he reasoned like this with himself: 'If there is a God, he would never have allowed this to happen; so as it did happen, there isn't a God.' But I have a suspicion that the postscript was a way of punishing God for letting it happen. Perhaps the writer was really saying, 'If God allows that kind of thing to happen, then I for one will refuse to believe in him — so there!' On the other hand a lot of people rather like to revive their belief in God at such a time because then they can off-load the terrible tragedy onto someone very remote from the scene. As one writer put it quite bluntly, 'It appeared that those who found no time for the church would wish to find a scapegoat in God.' This way we can duck learning lessons because it was all his fault anyway. I can understand people making these kind of responses in a moment of frustrated anger or despairing grief; but they are not very rational, are they? Children are notorious for off-loading blame. 'It wasn't me', says the youngster, covered from head to foot in mud, when mum demands to know who trampled dirt across the hall, 'it was someone else.' It always is. And when we become adults God is a good scapegoat because, so long as we do not listen in the right direction, he never answers back to defend himself.

In brief, then, we must place the blame for man-made disasters where it is due; but at the same time we must learn the lessons that God is teaching us through man's foolishness and weakness and we must draw from any tragedy the positive values and purposes that are always inherent within it. The Christian answer is positive, not negative. Just to throw out God, or throw off all the responsibility onto him, is neither honest nor reasonable. Nor is it very helpful. We must do better than that.

Natural disasters

St Pierre was a busy seaport and the commercial centre of the French island of Martinique, one of the Leeward Islands dividing the Atlantic Ocean from the Caribbean Sea. On 2 May 1902 a fine shower of white ash from Mt Pelée covered the town and the volcano rumbled its discontent. The following day lava flowed down the side of the mountain and earth tremors shook the town. Local government officials reassured the 30,000 inhabitants that there was no danger and the people were discouraged from evacuating the city. By 5 May Mt Pelée was glowing and the boiling mud and lava came nearer the town. Ants and snakes descended upon St Pierre and a massive wall of mud crushed a sugar refinery, slid into the harbour and caused a tidal wave that destroyed the waterfront buildings. In spite of the furious activity of Pelée and the loss of life and property in St Pierre the people were encouraged to remain calm. On Thursday morning, 8 May, the mountain fell silent and the sun shone. The city seemed at peace. Suddenly a huge red ball appeared on the side of the mountain and began to roll towards the

town. Just after 8 a.m. St Pierre was buried under a mountain of boiling lava and ash and 30,000 people had perished.

We may look back in amazement at the incredible stupidity of a people who ignored so many warnings, but we cannot blame the Coal Board or anyone else for the boiling mountain. The responsibility appears to stand with the Almighty alone; it was an 'act of God'. Like death itself these natural disasters affect all men sooner or later. But like death also, they do not just affect the really bad people; everyone, including little children, is involved.

These 'natural disasters' are the usual hunting-ground for those who attack the Christian faith. Man doesn't seem to be responsible at all, so the whole blame falls squarely upon God. As a Christian, how do I face up to this? Well, I do have an answer, but I may as well admit in advance that, though it is true, it is not very popular. The Bible everywhere teaches that God must and will punish sin. Christ claimed to have 'authority to judge' (John 5:27), Paul spoke of the day when 'God will judge men's secrets through Jesus Christ' (Romans 2:16). Hebrews 9:27 reminds us that man is 'destined to die once, and after that to face judgement'. James warns that 'Judgement without mercy will be shown to anyone who has not been merciful' (James 2:13). Peter looked on to a time when men 'will have to give account to him who is ready to judge the living and the dead' (1 Peter 4:5). John encouraged Christians with the reminder that they will have 'confidence on the day of judgement' (1 John 4:17). And Jude expected a day when the Lord would come 'to judge everyone' (Jude v.15). The result of that judgement for those who do not trust in Christ for salvation is almost

too terrible to describe. Writing to the Thessalonians, Paul referred to it in this way: 'They will be punished with everlasting destruction and shut out from the presence of the Lord and from the majesty of his power' (2 Thessalonians 1:9). John put the matter plainly when he wrote, 'If anyone's name was not found written in the book of life, he was thrown into the lake of fire' (Revelation 20:15).

The purpose of establishing the teaching of the Bible on the subject of the judgement is to make it clear that one day a final judgement will arrive from which no man will be exempt. It will be a day of terror for those who have rejected God and his Son. God must punish sin, to be consistent with the importance of his own laws. The punishment of God's final judgement is called hell: 'shut out from the presence of the Lord', says Paul. 'The lake of fire', says John. You may think that this is not really so bad. After all, if you seem to live fairly satisfactorily now without Christ, you ought to be able to manage without him in hell also. I can best explain the horror of hell and the joy of heaven by recalling that Christ left heaven and lived and died on this sinful earth in order that he might save us from hell and bring us to heaven. God knows what hell is like.

So, what has all this to do with natural disasters? Just this: every natural disaster is not merely a reminder of the immediate result of sin, but a solemn warning of the ultimate result of sin. The tragedy of St Pierre was not because the townsfolk were a more sinful people than anywhere else, but it was, and is, a serious warning that sin brings judgement from which none can escape. Natural disasters are the Day of Judgement written small. They are effectively God's trumpet sounding an alarm

that all is not well with the world, that man cannot control his world and that man is responsible and answerable to a God who punishes disobedience. The reason for the disaster is once again positive and constructive: it is intended to point man away from himself. It reinforces the New Testament claim that 'We brought nothing into the world, and we can take nothing out of it' (1 Timothy 6:7). The self-made man who, like the ancient city of Tyre, says, 'I am a god' (Ezekiel 28:2), is warned of the fragility of his empire, the transitory nature of all his glory and the inevitable judgement that is to come. The fact that very few heed the warning of God does not condemn God, but man. A parent will slap a disobedient child in the hope that such relatively mild punishment will avoid the need of more serious punishment later. Unfortunately, the raps of God make little impression upon man's rebellious and delinquent spirit. The severity of some natural disasters is God's alarm, warning man that worse is to come. His action in one part of the world is intended as a lesson to the whole world. No one will ever be able to stand before God and hide behind the excuse: 'I thought man was master of his own fate,' or 'You never warned me how seriously you viewed sin.' Without putting a fine point on it, if any man, living in today's world, really believes that man is in charge or that God winks at sin, he must be a fool. C. S. Lewis once referred to suffering as 'blockades on the road to hell'. Suffering ought to make us stop and think. These things do not just happen by chance.

During the battle of Waterloo the Scots Greys made a magnificent charge into the French lines; they cut their way through the artillery and swept many infantry from the field. Napoleon waited until the Greys were nearly exhausted before he ordered his lancers to countercharge.

The bugler from the English lines sounded the withdrawal, but the Scots Greys took no notice; drunk with victory, their sabres slashed out everywhere. Their strength exhausted, the cream of Wellington's cavalry realized too late that they could not escape and they were impaled by the French lancers. 'The finest cavalry in the world,' Napoleon is reputed to have commented, 'and the worst led.' Who was to blame? Wellington? His bugler? Or those who foolishly refused to listen to a warning and obey a command?

You may want to counter: 'Why does God have to be so severe? Why can't he ease off a little? Why in these natural disasters do so many have to suffer so badly?' If I am right in claiming that these tragedies are part of God's alarm, waking man from his godless indifference and warning him of a judgement to come, then we ought to take such 'acts of God' very seriously. If man was more open to the voice of God perhaps such extreme measures would not be necessary. But look at the United Kingdom. This nation is mercifully preserved from some of the horrifying catastrophes experienced elsewhere in the world. We have no volcanoes, no tornadoes, no significant earthquakes, relatively few floods and none of the magnitude of India or Pakistan. In 1976 Ingrid Holford wrote a book called *British Weather Disasters*. In this book she made the same point, that the British climate is, as she put it, 'comparatively equable'. Mrs Holford went on to say, 'Yet there are few disasters caused by the weather in other parts of the world which are not mirrored by similar events in Britain.' In other words, we have almost everything everybody else has, but on a very small scale. Now this means that as far as this country is concerned God *has* eased off a little. As a result, are we one of the

most God-fearing nations and especially open to the teaching of his Word? On the contrary, the United Kingdom is a godless and pagan society that generally ignores or ridicules the Scriptures. So, what effect does God's 'soft touch' have? It almost seems to encourage some men in sin.

When we read of a natural disaster and find ourselves saying, 'I can't believe in a God who lets that happen,' we should stop and ask ourselves what we would like God to do. Do we really want him to wink at man's sinful rebellion against his holy laws and never sound an alarm, reminding men of their sin, their weakness and the inevitability of judgement to come? It is no friend of mine who flatters and praises when I am heading for eternal disaster. Whenever I speak of natural disasters in this way I can usually expect someone to take up the challenge: 'That's all blackmail. God threatens me and says, "If you don't toe the line, this is what will happen to you one day." I'm not interested in a God who blackmails me.' Come off it! Is that what you shout at the lorry driver when his horn blasts you out of your day-dream just before you step under his wheels? 'Blackmail! I'm not interested.' Is that what you say to your doctor when he warns you of the need for an immediate operation as an alternative to inevitable death within a few months? 'Doctor, how dare you try to frighten me with blackmail?' Is that what you say of the British Rail notice threatening a fixed fine for improper use of the communication cord? Or the supermarket notice that thieves will be prosecuted? Or the notice that warns of high voltage cables, fast moving traffic, or oncoming vehicles in the middle of the road? Call it all blackmail if you like, but I for one would prefer to be told the truth. Given the reality of God and

the fact of a future judgement, God's red-letter signposts
in nature are part of his caring.

Ingrid Holford gave her reason for writing that book
about British weather disasters. It was not, she claimed, 'a
ghoulish interest in other people's misfortunes', but
because preventative measures are often inadequate:
'Many disasters', Ingrid Holford continued, 'have left the
uneasy feeling that blame does not entirely lie with the
weather but with man.' Mrs Holford was not writing a
Christian book at all; she was just facing facts. Sometimes
God is blamed for a disaster that is really made far worse
by man's stupidity. On 6 July 1973 the clouds tipped
118 mm. of rain onto Surbiton in two and a half hours.
The brook that normally drains rainwater from low-lying
streets in my locality was hindered by a blocked outlet and
the fire brigade pumping extra water into it from the
flooded A3 underpass! A small cul-de-sac nearby was
flooded to a depth of three feet and many elderly,
uninsured residents lost everything. Who was to blame?
Ingrid Holford commented, 'Heavy rain may be an "act
of God" but the provision of drains is a job for local
authorities.' The destruction of St Pierre in May 1902 was
made more horrendous for the same reason — the
ignorance or foolishness of man.

Who built the wall?

A member of staff was sitting in the common room
catching up with the news in his daily paper. A section of
the Berlin wall was pictured. It was at the time when the
East Germans were a little disappointed at the growing
number of their comrades who preferred life across the

border and so they were building the wall higher and
thicker. I was economizing by reading my colleague's
newspaper at a respectful distance! A master in the
French department pushed his way between us and
stubbed his finger at the photograph of the wall: 'See what
capitalism does,' he barked. 'Tom' was well known for his
strong political views backed by an atheistic philosophy,
and he probably really believed that the wall was intended
to keep the West Germans out; it was all the fault of
capitalism. Morning break had nearly gone and there was
no time for philosophic debate or political analysis before
we pitched into the next lesson. My friend looked up from
his paper, smiled quizzically at Tom and asked, 'Who
built the wall?' That question brushed theorizing aside
and placed the blame practically where it was due.

This century more than one hundred million people
have been killed in war. An impressive achievement by
man! Add to this the millions who every year die of
starvation, disease and exposure as a direct result of
man's selfish inhumanity and careless indifference to the
plight of his fellow men. I find it strange how often people
try to blame God for the world's starving millions. If God
had given us a world that had proved incapable of
supporting the four and a half thousand million mouths
that have to be fed, then he would be at fault. But as a
matter of fact there is plenty of food in the world to feed
everyone; it is only man's selfish greed that makes famines
hurt. When we look at the state of our world the finger
does not point at God. We must be honest and ask that
simple question: 'Who built the wall?' Who puts up the
barriers to love and co-operation and pity? God has given
man a blueprint on how to live; the Maker's instructions
are all found in the Bible and if we choose to ignore them

the walls go up and compassion crumbles. Tragedy results. Whose fault is that? before a man uses God as the scapegoat for the world's agony, he ought first to take a good look at himself to see how much he personally contributes towards the world's unhappiness. If you really want to know what man is capable of when God leaves him to himself, I suggest you read the story of the defence of Stalingrad in 1943 or, better still, Solzhenitsyn's *The Gulag Archipelago*. Ignoring the Maker's instructions encourages others to do the same and that is exactly how sin got started in this world. Most of the depressing items in this morning's news are the direct result of men saying, in one way or another, 'We know better than God, we don't need Him.' So when the barriers go up, 'Who built the wall?'

2.
Back to the starting-line

Have you ever watched a school race when it takes the starter three or four attempts to get the children off all at the same time? It happens right up to Olympic standard as well; there is always someone who is too eager to cross the line and get into the race and who leaves everyone standing before the race has begun! Perhaps you are already thinking that this book is a little like that. We jumped straight into the problems of today and you find yourself saying, 'Hold on a minute! It's all very well talking about disasters, but I want to ask a few questions that go back a bit.' Quite right! I have done what so many people do. We start with suffering and work back to God. But I do not think that is right at all. As a Christian I should start with God and his Word and move on to the problem of suffering. So, let me get back to the starting-line and we can start off from the same point and at the same pace.

When we set out to answer the question, 'Why suffering?' there are a few things we do well to keep clear in our minds; it will be a good thing not to forget them because they can save misunderstandings later.

First of all, the Christian lives in the same world as everyone else. I can listen to the same news items, watch the same programmes and read the same papers as you can. My anger can be roused by injustice, my heart

tortured by someone's suffering and my own body racked
by pain. I, too, can shed tears. Sometimes the question is
asked as if the Christian is quite unaware of the world in
which he lives; as if there must be an inevitable
contradiction between faith in God and facing up to the
harsh realities of life. I think he was being a little too
pessimistic, but George Orwell was not far away when he
wrote, back in 1950: 'Most people get a fair amount of fun
out of their lives, but on balance life is suffering, and only
the very young or the very foolish imagine otherwise.' The
Christian is a realist; he sees the world and its problems
and faces up to them. He is neither like the ostrich nor the
giraffe, neither refusing to face up to life, nor overlooking
it. The very fact that there are Christians in today's world
of suffering and violence is proof enough that facing the
facts and believing in a God of love are not mutually
exclusive. After all, long before George Orwell looked at
life, Eliphaz was reminding poor Job that 'Man is born to
trouble as surely as sparks fly upward' (Job 5:7).
Christians are involved in war and pain, suffering and
injustice, earthquakes and famines, like everyone else,
and they still believe in a God of love. You may think they
are all children or foolish, but on the other hand they may
have found the answer.

There is something else we should keep in view.
Sometimes the question about suffering comes sincerely
and searchingly, but often it comes like a broadsword to
cut away the Christian's faith and bleed his belief in God
to death. In reply Christians often argue as if they only
had a shield to fight with; they are on the defence at once.
They talk about this 'mystery' and commonly agree that
all the suffering in the world must make even the stout-
hearted Christian doubt occasionally. Oscar Wilde,

hardly noted for his Christian convictions, once wrote, 'Clergymen and people who use phrases without wisdom sometimes talk of suffering as a mystery. It is really a revelation.' I do not know what he meant by that, but it sounds positive and not defensive. I know how I understand that phrase of Wilde's, and if he meant what I believe it to mean, then he was right! This book is not written on the defensive. I am convinced that the Christian answer to the question of suffering is positive and hopeful.

Having said this, however, there is a third and very important point I must stress. While it is true that the Christian is not on the defensive on this issue, hiding behind the 'mystery' of God's dealing in the world as if that closed all further legitimate discussion, we must nevertheless insist that we do not have slick and easy answers to every question. The Christian believes that God is all-powerful, all-wise and all-holy; this means he never makes a mistake and everything he does is right and just. On the other hand, the Christian also believes that man is sinful and fallible. Therefore it is really impertinent of man to put God in the dock. Who do we think we are, to make God explain everything to us and justify his actions? In the Old Testament God listened to Job and his friends arguing about suffering and then broke in with this challenge: 'Who is this that darkens my counsel with words without knowledge? Brace yourself like a man; I will question you, and you shall answer me. Where were you when I laid the earth's foundation? Tell me, if you understand. Who marked off its dimensions? Surely you know! Who stretched a measuring line across it? On what were its footings set, or who laid its cornerstone — while the morning stars sang together and all the angels shouted

for joy?' (Job 38: 2–7.) Through Isaiah God put the point even more plainly: 'Whom did the Lord consult to enlighten him, and who taught him the right way? Who was it that taught him knowledge or showed him the path of understanding?' (Isaiah 40:14.)

I can hear you thinking,'That's a cop out; he's going to duck every issue by a nice pious statement that we must not question God.' No, I am never going to use this argument again in this book. We will face every challenge and attempt an answer to every question, but you ought to know that for the Christian the whole debate is carried on with a reverent respect for the sovereign God in whom he believes. You don't have to be a Christian to believe that man is finite. No man knows everything, and if you put together all the wisdom of all men who have ever lived, that super-knowledge would not know everything either! No branch of science has exhausted its possibilities, so we can hardly expect man to touch the outer perimeters of metaphysics — let alone the 'deep things of God'. This is not to close up discussion, but to put man and God in perspective. The one is finite, the other is infinite, and that should make us at least a little cautious. I am not trying to defend God; that would be unnecessary. I am not trying to explain all his ways; that would be presumptuous. But I am trying to explain the Christian viewpoint, and this will be done against the background of a firm belief in a God who is holy and just.

Where do we begin?

The Christian's starting-point is God. To avoid God leaves life without an ultimate purpose and the question

we are faced with here without an ultimate answer. You
may not be convinced that there is a God, but that doesn't
mean you are wasting time with this book. All I ask is that
you try to see things as the Christian sees them. Some
people dismiss the Christian's answer to suffering as
'nonsense' just because they cannot accept the Christian's
belief in a wise and personal God. But that is not very fair.
You may never accept my view of God — that is your
prerogative — but, given my firm conviction that there is
a God, my arguments may be positive and rational. Try to
keep this in mind; after all, you have to do the same thing,
don't you? You have to find an answer to suffering from
your premise of 'no God'. Accepting each other's
premise, we are really discussing who can make the most
sense out of suffering. And to start with God we must
begin with the Bible. Once again you may respond, 'But I
don't believe the Bible.' Fair enough, we all have the right
not to believe, but if you want to hear a Christian's answer
you must at least let him use his own basic source-book
for his argument. You cannot ask a Communist what his
political philosophy is and then refuse to let him quote
from the *Communist Manifesto*. Similarly, if you want to
know the theology of Islam you will expect a Moslem to
turn to the *Koran*. Now, as a matter of fact, the Christian
does not talk of the Bible merely as another book. It is
not. It is unique because it is God's Word and is entirely to
be trusted in all its statements. If the Christian does not
start there, he might as well abandon any attempt to make
sense out of life. If he cannot trust the Bible everywhere,
he cannot trust it anywhere. It is because men have
tailored the *Manifesto* to suit their own ideas and
situations that it is virtually impossible to ask for the
'Communist view' about anything. The answer will

depend upon the faction of Communism you are speaking
to. The same is true of Islam and sadly, of 'Christianity'
also. Where there are differences in major areas the
reason is always the same: the disciples of Marx,
Muhammed or Christ have altered the 'source book' to
suit themselves. Marx and Muhammed were men; they
claimed no more, and we may feel free, therefore, to
criticize. But Christ was God and he stamped the Bible
with his approval. This is the Christian starting-point.

But in the argument of this book I am not asking the
unbeliever to perform mental contortions and pretend to
himself that he really believes what he is sure is not true.
You cannot reason yourself all the way into Christianity,
for it is essentially a matter of faith, but Christianity is
perfectly reasonable. I have spent hours explaining my
faith to people, defending my arguments, trying hard to
convince them that what I am saying is absolutely right,
while all the time I know that I will never argue them into
the Christian life. A man becomes a Christian by faith,
and faith is a gift of God. But still I argue and discuss
because faith and reason are not opposites. Reason is like
a distress flare in a ship. The mariner can sail for years
without a flare, but it might save him a lot of trouble
sooner or later if he takes one along; and to take a flare
with him is not an admission of bad seamanship. When I
say that my faith is reasonable it means simply that my
faith can be talked over and thought through; faith does
not stop a man asking questions, nor does it insult his
intelligence. What all this means for the question in front
of us is simply this: you do not have to believe either in
God or the Bible to go on reading. Think over the
arguments and weigh them up; if they are truth they will
speak for themselves. And if at the end you disagree, then

be honest enough to put up a better alternative.

Where it all began

Let me tell you a story. There was once a boy who was given by his father a beautiful garden. It was everything a boy could wish for. There were rivers and streams and ponds in this garden, with islands and rock pools. It was a large garden. Fruit trees of all kinds grew here — pears and apples, plums and cherries, grapes and oranges and large sweet strawberries as well. It was a garden full of beautiful butterflies and birds and flowers, and the animals were all tame. The sun always shone, and the rain was warm and clean. It was always summertime.

It was a real paradise. Each night the boy could return to his father's home. There was no hard work to be done, everything just grew; there were no weeds or stinging nettles to spoil it. The boy was strong and healthy and he enjoyed the garden. There was just one warning that the father had given. The boy could go anywhere and enjoy everything, but he must never light a fire. Now the boy was quite happy with this condition and for a long time enjoyed all the beauty and fun of the garden. He loved his father and often played with him in the garden and thanked him for such a wonderful gift.

One day the boy stopped playing and thought about that warning. Like all boys he was adventurous and began to consider it an annoying warning. Why not just a small fire? It would be fun to cook apples and stew plums. He would be very careful; he would not play with fire. Surely there could be no harm? He gathered dry grass, small twigs and some large logs of wood and set everything in

order in a little clearing in the centre of the garden. The grass and twigs burnt well and he piled on the logs. The fire grew bigger and bigger and the flames leapt into the sky. Thrilled with his success, the boy stacked more wood onto his fire. A flame leapt into a nearby tree and set light to some of the lower branches. The boy ran to the river with a bucket to put out the flames, but when he returned the fire had spread and was eating up the grass and trees around him. He ran to the river to escape the heat; but the fire reached the river and leapt across to the other side. The boy ran and ran but could not escape. The flames swept across the beautiful garden until everything was reduced to ashes. The boy escaped with his life but was badly burned.

He was afraid and ashamed to meet his father and ran to hide; but there was nowhere to hide and his father found him. When he was sufficiently recovered, the boy set out to make a new garden of his own, like the first one. But it was never the same. He worked hard and long; he dug and raked and planted. But the weeds and thistles choked his efforts. He became bad-tempered and angry. The animals fled from him and fought among themselves. Other children came to the garden and sometimes played, but mostly they fought and quarrelled. They never went back to the father's house, not even at night; they no longer cared for the father. The father looked on sadly. No one asked his advice; no one went to him for help.

I will stop the story there because maybe there is already a vaguely familiar ring about it! When God first made a man and a woman he put them on a world that he said was good. He settled them in a special garden that he had prepared. Everything was perfect and there was no evil in the heart of Adam, no disorder in creation, and

nature was in perfect harmony with itself. According to Genesis 1:26, God made man in his own 'image and likeness'. This does not refer to man's physical appearance but to the fact that man, like his Maker, is a moral being who is rational and responsible for his actions. We all recognize this when we put men on trial for their crimes. If my dog bites you, it would be absurd to stand him in front of a magistrate for cross-examination. It is me you will prosecute and the magistrate might simply order the dog to be shot! But this 'image and likeness' is also seen in man's desire and ability to worship. Wherever we find men, we find them worshipping. However primitive and misguided, men must worship because, as St Augustine wrote sixteen hundred years ago, 'Our soul is restless until it finds its rest in thee.' Dogs do not say prayers, but men do. When Adam and Eve were first created 'God made mankind upright' (Ecclesiastes 7:29). This word 'upright' does not mean they were morally neutral; it implies that they were glad to worship God and serve him and had no inclination to sin. When God came 'walking in the garden in the cool of the day', Adam and Eve were ready to meet with Him. This was not an innocency of ignorance, because Adam was not simply aware of the blessings of obedience, he was also warned of the judgement upon disobedience. Speaking of the forbidden tree, God plainly said, 'When you eat of it you will surely die' (Genesis 2:17).

Evidently disease and death were no part of God's perfect plan for mankind; certainly in the garden Adam would 'work it and take care of it' (Genesis 2:15) but this would involve no great effort or hard labour: 'Streams came up from the earth and watered the whole surface of the ground. And the Lord God formed man from the dust

of the ground and breathed into his nostrils the breath of
life, and man became a living being. Now the Lord God
had planted a garden in the east, in Eden; and there he put
the man he had formed. And the Lord God made all kinds
of trees grow out of the ground — trees that were pleasing
to the eye and good for food. In the middle of the garden
were the tree of life and the tree of the knowledge of good
and evil' (Genesis 2:6–9). Although Isaiah 11:6–9 has a
poetic application to the new spiritual life Christ gives, it
may well reflect the actual state of affairs that, without
Adam's sin, would have continued in the Garden of Eden:
'The wolf will live with the lamb, the leopard will lie down
with the goat, the calf and the lion and the yearling
together; and a little child will lead them. The cow will
feed with the bear, their young will lie down together, and
the lion will eat straw like the ox. The infant will play near
the hole of the cobra, and the young child put his hand
into the viper's nest. They will neither harm nor destroy
on all my holy mountain, for the earth will be full of the
knowledge of the Lord as the waters cover the sea.'

Everything was perfect and good and there was just
nothing to spoil the enjoyment of Adam and Eve. God
was ready for all mankind to share this because he told
our first parents: 'Be fruitful and increase in number; fill
the earth and subdue it. Rule over the fish of the sea and
the birds of the air and over every living creature that
moves on the ground' (Genesis 1:28). Remember, Adam
and Eve served God out of love; they worshipped him
freely and not by compulsion. They were not puppets. At
that time they were really free. God made them free.

Now let's pause a moment and think about this. So
many people seem to imagine that pain and misery and
violence have always been part of man's lot and that God

made it this way. Not so, says the Bible. Whatever the outcome of the story, one thing is clear: God made a good world and put two perfect people in it. They loved and obeyed God out of free choice and they enjoyed God's creation at its very best. There was nothing to spoil it. The Christian can therefore claim a reason for his optimism and hope. If this is how God started it all, there is a strong possibility that he has some good plans for the future, especially if he has given us evidence of those plans. Think of the alternative. It is no part of this discussion to debate the various views of the origin of man, but to say the least it is rather depressing to think that the present day suffering and evil are the inevitable results of that first blob of something that hauled itself out of the mud and sunned itself dry on the land. According to such a view of man an honest look at history tells us man never will get better. If you do not accept the Bible account, there is not even a glimmer of hope on the horizon; man has always been bad and that is all there is to it. His chemical composition and his history are against any future hope.

The Christian viewpoint also starts positively. Man has not always been what he is. He had a good start, a perfect beginning and, speaking generally, man has never quite lost his longing to get back to where he was. Man longs for peace and happiness and security, and woven into the fabric of his soul is a distant recollection that a man can know God and find peace. Someone has described history as 'the autobiography of a madman' and without the Christian viewpoint that is about all that can be said.

What spoilt it all?

In the garden God had placed a tree. He called it 'the tree
of the knowledge of good and evil' (Genesis 2:17). The
tree was not necessarily a special or unusual tree and it
certainly did not bear a 'charmed' fruit. What was
significant about it was that it represented a test of their
love and obedience. God had put a ban on this tree alone;
it was his first negative command, or prohibition, to
created man. But he was not trying to catch out Adam and
Eve or trip them up. His purpose was to ensure that if the
human race was to go on loving God it would do so out of
loyal obedience and not from blind ignorance. He wanted
man to love him freely. For this reason he gave Adam an
alternative, a choice. But you may object, 'Imagine a
father having several bottles of different sweets, who
includes one bottle with poisonous pills and tells his child
that he can take the sweets from all the bottles except from
this particular one; he knows very well that if the child
disobeys then the consequences could be really serious.
Surely a loving father would not let that happen;
particularly when he knows that his enemy (Satan) is
going to disguise himself as a kind and lovable man and
tempt and deceive the child to take those tablets. Would a
loving father assess the affection and loyalty of his child
by subjecting the child to such a dangerous and
precarious test?'

This story, however, is not parallel because it presumes
that Adam and Eve were children with very little
understanding and even less personal responsibility.
Innocence does not imply ignorance. They knew God
personally. The friendship and relationship between man
and God *before* the Fall was based upon a regular walking

with God in the garden. The innocence of Adam and Eve
with regard to sin was the result of this close and very
personal relationship with God. Because of this, we
cannot compare the forbidden tree to a bottle of
poisonous pills placed among several jars of sweets;
Adam and Eve were perfectly capable of understanding
God's command and appreciating the consequences of
disobedience. A closer parallel would be the thousands of
parents today who, in growing a beautiful garden
necessarily grow within it some lovely shrubs, flowers and
trees, parts of which are poisonous. The parents give
specific instructions to the family regarding the nature of
the fruits to be avoided and the consequences of
disobeying this order; the older and thus the more
responsible the children are, then the more the parents
expect to trust them. The alternative would be to bulldoze
the garden and put it all down to lettuces! It was not a
'dangerous and precarious test', but a reasonable way of
proving the loyalty of our first parents.

Sadly, man made the wrong choice. He ate from the
forbidden tree, and sin, disobedience to God, came into
his life and into the world. The story of this 'Fall',
recorded in Genesis 3, is not a myth or fable; the Bible
claims it actually happened that way. Isaiah referred to it
seven hundred years before Christ: 'Your first father
sinned' (Isaiah 43:27), and so did Hosea, preaching at the
same time as Isaiah: 'Like Adam, they have broken the
covenant' (Hosea 6:7). Christ himself spoke of Adam and
Eve in Matthew 19:4, and Paul referred to Adam in
1 Corinthians 15:22: 'For as in Adam all die, so in Christ
all will be made alive', and to Eve in 2 Corinthians 11:3: 'I
am afraid that just as Eve was deceived by the serpent's
cunning, your minds may somehow be led astray from

your sincere and pure devotion to Christ.'

What happened next is nothing short of disaster. God had warned Adam and Eve of the consequences of disobedience and now he carried out his threat. They were driven out of the garden, and the world they now faced was hostile. Death, pain and hard work became part of the common life of Adam and his descendants. You can read in Genesis 3:16–19 some of the immediate results of the Fall. But worse is yet to be told. When man first fell into sin, it was not just his outward circumstances that changed but his whole nature. In the New Testament Paul wrote a letter to the Christians at Rome and he described carefully the state of man since the Fall.

Man's will is in rebellion against the truth: 'Men suppress the truth by their wickedness' (Romans 1:18).

Man's mind is without ultimate purpose: 'Their thinking became futile' (Romans 1:21).

Man's heart is without love for God: 'They neither glorified him as God' (Romans 1:21).

Man's conscience is corrupted: 'They not only continue to do these very things [things opposed to God's law] but also approve of those who practise them' (Romans 1:32).

Man's emotions are out of control: 'God gave them over in the sinful desires of their hearts ...' (Romans 1:24).

Man's will, mind, heart, conscience and emotions are all spoiled by sin. It is not that all men are as bad as they possibly can be; most of us could be worse than we are! Nor does it mean that man is incapable of doing good or appreciating beauty; but it does mean that man is spoiled by sin and is slanted away from God in every part of his nature. Man is totally out of line with God. The image of God that we spoke about earlier is not entirely lost, but it

is severely damaged. God created man in mint condition, but sin has seriously defaced him. Satan vandalized man.

When man fell into sin he lost his freedom. It is commonplace to hear people talking about man's free will; they say man can decide whether or not to sin, he has a perfect freedom. As the philosopher Henley put it, 'I am the master of my fate, I am the captain of my soul.' We must put away this idea of freedom once and for all. We are not born free; we are bound to sin, we just can't help it. But before you cry out, 'Nonsense,' let me prove it to you. Whenever someone tells me they have a free will I reply, 'Then let me give you a very simple task, and with the exercise of your free will I am sure you will have no difficulty in accomplishing it. I want you to live the next seven days as perfectly as Christ himself. I want you to make up your mind to be absolutely perfect in thoughts, words and actions, so that you obey your conscience in everything and God's Word right down to the letter. Now just do this for seven days, and then let me come and talk to you, and also those you live with, just to check up that you really have been such a perfect person!' To date no one has ever taken me up on this. They usually smile and concede the point. Man lost his freedom in the garden of Eden. He is free to sin, but he is not free not to sin. This is surely the most terrible fact about the violence of today's world: man just cannot help it. That does not excuse him, but it does explain him.

'Cursed is the ground because of you.' Those terrible words of God to Adam in Genesis 3:17 tell us of something else that happened at the Fall. When sin came into the life of man, the whole natural order of the universe shuddered as a result. Creation was affected. Paul says in Romans 8:20, 'The creation was subjected to

frustration.' The word 'frustration' means 'uselessness, purposelessness'. He goes on to speak of creation 'groaning as in the pains of childbirth' and waiting to be 'liberated from its bondage to decay'. All this is a picture of a world out of harmony, in some kind of disorder. When we look around at creation there is a paradox of order and chaos:

> The seasons come and go,
> A time to reap and sow,
> Plants die and grow,
> Rain, sun and snow.

But then nature seems to go mad and the order is broken. The earth splits, mountains spit fire, snow falls in July! Not just man, but all creation has been spoiled by sin. That, according to the Christian, is how it all began. And that is where our problem begins as well.

3.
Isn't God a bit hard?

Tom shifted painfully in his chair. 'I know', he said with a half smile, 'you've said all this to me before; but look here, if I was all-powerful and in charge of everything I wouldn't just sit back and let little children starve. I couldn't stand by and watch innocent people being beaten to death. So what kind of God is it who lets these things happen?' Tom had spent so much time in and out of hospital that he knew the meaning of suffering. What troubled him was not simply his own pain, but that his life was often surrounded by those whose life and limbs were just not working properly and many of them suffered intensely.

Why start it all?

No Christian can deny that God knew what the result would be if he gave Adam and Eve a free choice. They did not have to sin, but they chose to sin, and God knew this would happen. He also knew all about the misery that would follow. So why didn't God stop Adam and Eve from sinning, or make the punishment lighter, or why did he bother to make them at all? A handful of angels could have looked after the earth and kept it all in trim.

But to suggest God should have made it impossible for

Adam and Eve to sin is to miss the point made in the previous chapter. I said there, 'God wanted to ensure that if the human race was to go on loving God it would do so out of loyal obedience and not from blind ignorance. He wanted man to love him freely. For this reason he gave Adam an alternative, a choice.' We also made the point in the last chapter that whereas at the moment of his temptation Adam was free to choose right or wrong, obedience or disobedience, righteousness or sin, once he had yielded to the temptation sin came into man's life and he is no longer free. God let man start free.

Have you noticed that the people who try passionately to defend their 'free will' are the very ones who criticize God for allowing Adam and Eve freedom to choose? Strange, isn't it? It reminds me of the fact that in our society the people most critical of the forces of law and order are usually the most vocal in demanding their 'rights'. Perhaps this tells us something about human nature since the Fall! 'God will never force you to do anything.' That is quite a widely held view, isn't it? Like many popular views, it is not altogether right, but those who argue in its favour usually suggest God would be unjust to compel man to do anything. You cannot defend man's freedom and at the same time suggest it was unfair of God to allow Adam to choose freely whether or not to obey him.

You may reply, 'All right, I accept the value of that first free choice, but look at the mess that results from it. Why did God have to make the punishment so severe, and why let it affect every generation?' Sometimes I stumble across parents who really cannot believe their children are sinful by nature, that they have a natural bias to disobedience. This is what the Christian calls 'original sin'. Some people

hate the idea of 'original sin'. But I have never yet met any parents who admit that their child was such a perfect angel that they actually taught it one or two naughty things just to make it normal! We spend all our lives teaching children to be good; badness is something we never have to teach them; it is just there! So, whether or not we like the phrase 'original sin', it is sadly an established fact. The Bible has no doubt about it. David complained, 'Surely I have been a sinner from birth, sinful from the time my mother conceived me' (Psalm 51:5). Sin is a matter of what we are, not what we learn. James put it this way: 'Each one is tempted when, by his own evil desire, he is dragged away and enticed' (James 1:14). After a generation of spoon-feeding the nation's children and youth, Sweden has learned this lesson the hard way. Jerzy Sarnecki, an expert in juvenile delinquency at the National Council of Crime Prevention in Sweden, has come to this conclusion: 'We have learned that it is a sociologist's myth to imagine that people are not fundamentally responsible for their own crimes.'

But wasn't it all a bit hard of God? He didn't have to make a sinful nature something we all inherit, did he? No, he didn't have to, but in doing so he has taught us a lesson that we could learn in no other way. Original sin, the inherited sinful nature with which we are all born, teaches us that sin is not something personal, just between me and myself or even between me and God. When a man sets out to be unfaithful to his wife, or to falsify his tax or expense records, or to pilfer the petty cash, he thinks that it will never affect anyone else. Sooner or later he learns that it always does. Sin will out. No man sins to himself; it always affects others. But this is no startlingly new discovery. If only man would listen, original sin has been

teaching this to man ever since Cain and Abel were born. Parents who watch their darling kicking the paper off the wall in a tantrum ought not to excuse him and console themselves with the fact that 'he will grow out of it'. As a matter of fact, he will not grow out of it: he will simply replace a childish expression of sin by an adult one. The parents ought to be asking a much more serious question, namely: 'Why is he like this? Where did that temper come from?' And the answer to that question does not depend upon a family search into the characters and habits of the paternal and maternal grandparents. The answer is much simpler than that. It goes back to the Fall and reminds us that sin has very serious consequences. Original sin is therefore not God arbitrarily venting his anger against generations of poor unborn innocents, but it is his way of reminding every generation that sin, all sin, has tragic and far-reaching results. Without original sin man would not bother too much how he lived. He could always leave it to the next generation to put everything right. And knowing human nature as we do, every generation *would* leave the next one to 'put everything right'.

What we are saying, to express it another way, is this: original sin teaches us that there is a moral and spiritual continuity in the human race and that every generation affects the one that follows. This is an inescapable fact, whether or not you believe in original sin; it is just that original sin teaches it more clearly than anything else. And while we are on this subject we must not imagine that even if we believe that each new generation is totally free to make its own choice we have solved the problem. Have you ever found a satisfactory reason why so far no generation has ever made the right choice to obey God in everything and turn the clock back to Adam and Eve

before the Fall? If you reply that this is because each generation learns bad habits from the generation before it, then at least we are agreed that our children do not have a free will; they are bound to copy us.

All this from one little slip

But even allowing that this passing on of a sinful nature from one generation to the next has an important lesson to teach us, it does not quite answer the question: 'Isn't this rather hard of God? Surely he could teach that lesson an easier way! Besides, you cannot really maintain that the terrible suffering in today's world is justified by one little slip of Adam and Eve.' This is really two questions, not one, so we will take them separately.

Certainly God can teach us about the continuity of the human race apart from an inherited sinful nature. As a matter of fact, he does this in the realm of physical hereditary features: red hair runs in the family, and so on. But that is trivial compared with sin. Pigs and parrots have hereditary characteristics, but that tells us nothing about morality. Man refuses to learn the serious lesson God *does* give him, so he is hardly likely to think about the consequences of his sin just because he observes that all his sons and grandsons have brown eyes like himself. No, there really is no other way that can teach man so vividly the appalling consequences of sin, and without this lesson no one will take the sin problem seriously.

The other part of the question implies that all the suffering in the world is God getting his own back on Adam. That is plainly not so. It is true that, as Paul says, 'Sin entered the world through one man,' but he goes on

to claim, 'All sinned' (Romans 5:12). The suffering of today's world is the result of Adam's sin perpetuated by today's generation. The modern automobile is the cause of massive environmental pollution and thousands of gruesome accidents each year, but it is hardly just to blame Karl Benz, who in 1885 produced one of the first cars to be driven by the internal combustion engine. *We* are the people who build them, drive them and crash them today; not Karl Benz, or Gottlieb Daimler, or Henry Ford. You can blame Adam for starting the fire, but it is today's world that is piling on the fuel.

Do you notice the way people often talk about that first disobedience of man? 'One little slip' is how it is frequently described, and expressed like that it really does seem that God has taken a monolithic mountain of misery to crack down on a hiccup in the righteousness of Adam. But that 'one little slip' was a wilful violation of God's holy law, a despising of his promises and blessings, and it cast a serious question mark over the integrity of God's Word. 'Did God really say?' tempted Satan and then he came out with it: 'You will not surely die,' and Adam believed Satan rather than God. That was not a 'slip'; it was an open declaration of war against God. In effect Adam said by his action, 'God is a liar; Satan is true. God is cruel; Satan is kind.' And that is turning truth on its head. God had warned Adam concerning the special tree: 'When you eat of it you will surely die' and Adam's response said, 'Who cares? Come and try.' We do not allow men to react like that to our civil laws, so why should God be less concerned to uphold his law? Sin is serious, God says so, and the suffering in the world today is largely because man says sin does not matter.

It may be objected that when a man violates civil law,

for example, when he drives a car while drunk, he knows the danger he is in and there is much evidence of the consequences of such an action. We are never asked to obey blindly civil law; everyone can see the reason behind it. But could Adam see any reason for the ban on the tree? This argument, of course, is based upon the experience of a fallen sinful world. Adam *ought* to have trusted God simply because he knew sufficient about God to persuade him that the Creator is not arbitrary in his laws; he has a reason behind them all. Besides, God had plainly said, 'When you eat of it you will surely die.' That was a very good reason for Adam to be obedient.

Why cannot God forgive and forget?

Let us suppose God had winked at this declaration of war by Adam. Suppose God had taken a lesson from the softies today and had decided to let it all pass by. He would forgive and forget. Would that have brought Adam to his senses? No, it would have confirmed Satan's suggestion that God does not mean what he says. But it would also have done something else. It would have implied that man can sin as much as he likes and get away with it. It is well known that the greatest deterrent to crime is the strong possibility of being caught. In other words, it is not the law that frightens off the potential criminal, nor even the threat of punishment, but the likelihood of being found out. The more certain it is that a particular crime will be 'cracked', the less likely it is that the criminal will embark upon that course. If men could sin with impunity, it would simply encourage them to violate God's laws. When Hans Nestius set out in the

1960s to liberate Sweden from all laws restraining sex he really believed that his 'sex revolution' would cause sexual crimes to decrease, hard pornography to lose its appeal and prostitution simply to fade away. Without law and punishment and with total freedom as the alternative, men and women would enjoy sex without its violence and 'shameful dirt', as Nestius called it. Twenty years on, this 'freedom fighter' admits he was tragically wrong and has misled a whole generation. Sweden's crime rate for violent sexual offences increases alarmingly each year and the country leads the world in hard pornography, which Nestius refers to as 'such filth you would not believe'. A soft option will never make saints out of sinners. It is often only the fear of the consequences that holds men back from a profligate life. So it is for man's own good that God does not wink at sin. In society we expect crime to be brought to book. That is precisely what suffering is to man's sin: it brings him to book.

If God had winked at sin and patted Adam benevolently on the head with a few divine tuts, there is something else it would have achieved. Not only would it have encouraged man to think he can sin and get away with it, but it would have implied that God's laws were not really too important. What would we say of a magistrate who felt particularly generous one week and dismissed every case that came before him? He said he was feeling happy and wanted everyone else to feel the same! We would rightly demand that he be dismissed from the bench. We would remind him that he is there to uphold the law and that without punishments the law becomes a mockery. In all the debates about crime and punishment it is not often appreciated that the first and most important purpose of punishment is to vindicate the law.

Punishment may have the secondary purpose of discouraging the potential criminal and reforming the actual criminal, but these are not the chief purpose of punishment. Punishment, the suffering that follows the offence, is society's way of saying, 'The law matters, and we disapprove strongly of your violation of the law.' Many youngsters come out of our juvenile courts laughing at the law and the magistrate because, once again, they have got off 'scot free'. They do not need to take the law seriously because they have gained the impression that society doesn't really care about its laws. God cares about his laws and the punishment and suffering that follow the disobeying of them are God's way of saying, 'My laws are very important and if you break them, I warn you, things will go wrong.' The parent, teacher or society that makes idle threats will never gain respect for regulations.

Why not start again?

I don't know what you are like at maths, but when I was at school a sheet of my algebraic equations could easily have passed off as an example of a first-century Athenian schoolboy practising his alphabet; my sheet was often so crossed and blotted and generally spoilt that I had no alternative than to scrap it all and start again. Looking at the results of the Fall, why didn't God scrap man and start again? Of course, at one point he did. You can read the story of the flood in Genesis 6 to 8, but the eight survivors soon went back to the old disobedient ways that necessitated the flood in the first place. Ah! But you will say, 'They still had the old sinful nature of Adam after the

Fall. Why didn't God start right from the beginning with an Adam and Eve Mark II?' And if I suggest that *they* may have made the same wrong decision as the first pair, you will counter this with the possibility that God could have kept on repeating the experiment until eventually a couple got it right. Well, you can go further than this if you want to. Since God knows everything, he could have missed out all those who would have disobeyed and simply started with the pair whom he knew would obey! We have reduced the discussion almost to absurdity now, for this line of argument reduces man to a mere plaything of God. It is rather like the boy standing up skittles only to knock them all down again or, more seriously, the dictator using people as pawns in his game of power and pleasure. God does not toss man aside like a cat tormenting a helpless bird. He made man in his own image and likeness and therefore decided to allow man to run his course, putting him in a generally pleasant world, 'so that men would seek him and perhaps reach out for him and find him' (Acts 17:27). Unlike man's attitude to man, God treats mankind with respect and dignity and not as a plaything.

We would be outraged at the thought of parents killing their children as soon as they showed the first hint of disobedience. And even if we were told that our children would go on being disobedient as they grow up, we would still let them live and would bend our energies to control and contain their wild nature. This is precisely what God does. He allowed man in his disobedient infancy to live, and planned a way to change his wild nature. Christ described it as being 'born again' (John 3:3), and Paul claimed that 'If anyone is in Christ, he is a new creation; the old has gone, the new has come' (2 Corinthians 5:17). Once again this is where the Christian answer to suffering

has a positive note. God has offered man a salvation that involves a new birth, a new start for those who will trust in Christ. Even this new birth does not eradicate all the effects of sin in man's experience, but Paul could say to the young Christians at Philippi, 'He who began a good work in you will carry it on to completion until the day of Christ Jesus' (Philippians 1:6). God is always ready to start again with those who come to him in faith. It is a mark of his love that he does not simply blot out man as soon as he sins.

Is God the author of sin?

When the Christian talks about a firm belief in the all-powerful God and the conversation drifts on to the subject of creation and the Fall and the entrance of sin, it is not long before someone declares, 'Then that makes God responsible for sin, doesn't it?' This is a tough question and many Christians flinch from it. It is not that we do not know the answer. There can be no doubt about that! The problem lies rather in the fact that we do not know how to make our answer reasonable. If God were the author of sin, then he would be the devil, and not God. According to Christ it is Satan who is 'a murderer from the beginning . . . and the father of lies' (John 8:44). God did not invent or create sin and therefore cannot be its author. That dubious honour belongs to Satan who, as a created angel, rebelled against God, was turned out of heaven and continues his evil opposition to God on earth.

Then why did God make this 'angel who fell'? Or, having made him, why didn't he blot him out at once? After all, God sees the end from the beginning and he

knew the mess that Satan would make of the world God had made. This is an old question and a hard one. At the opening of the Synod at Cambridge, Massachusetts on 9 June 1647, the English settlers included a sermon in the Algorquim language for the benefit of the new Indian converts to Christianity. Following the sermon, we are told, the Indians were eager with their questions which included this one: 'Why did God not kill the devil that made all men to be bad, God having all power?'

The answer cannot lie in God's inability; it must rest, therefore, in his unwillingness. But why? In the last chapter we defended the freedom of choice God gave to Adam, even though he knew the result; God did not want puppets to worship him, but people. The same must be true of the angels in heaven. Some used their freedom to love and serve God, while others used it to hate and rebel. Having decided to allow the devil to continue in existence, in spite of the evil that would result, God set about curtailing and setting limits to his power. It is quite clear from the Bible that the devil is already limited in his power and authority. He could not harm Job without the permission of God (Job 1:12). Christ came to begin the work of destroying the power of the devil (1 John 3:8) and God has pledged himself to a time when the devil will no longer deceive, and all the results of his evil will be at an end (Revelation 20:10). In other words, all the evil and suffering that God allows on the earth is only for a limited duration; it is not for ever. The devil is not all-powerful, God has seen to that. Freedom may mean that he is free to deceive and men are free to believe him, but it does not mean that he will always be free.

When we view man's history, a history motivated, so often, by satanic forces, many of us appreciate the value

of God and consequently worship him in a way we would never do without the knowledge and experience of the results of the devil's freedom. The comfortable enjoyment of a warm summer is the more pleasant when it follows the cruel severity of a hard winter. I appreciate health all the more when it is restored after illness. Perhaps, as a Christian, I will understand the freedom of heaven in a way that would be impossible if it did not follow the so-called freedom of earth. This is why God has let the devil live a little longer.

However, if God is not exactly the author of sin, then surely he is at least responsible for it? Do you remember Tom's challenge at the beginning of this chapter? 'What kind of a God is it who lets these things happen?' If I stand by and watch a blind man walk into the path of a lorry, I could defend myself by claiming that I did not tell him to cross the road, nor was I driving the lorry. All quite true, but not very convincing, especially if I could have shouted or pulled him back; so I must bear some responsibility for his death. There is no escaping this conclusion. God did not create Adam blind, and he warned him very clearly of the danger of stepping out into the road. He could have placed the man in a harness and kept him on a short lead. The danger of letting the man walk free was the possibility of an accident, but we have already seen that the dignity of man necessitated that first free choice.

God is not therefore responsible for sin as its author; he did not invent it, cause it or even will it. But we cannot deny that he is responsible if by that we mean he allows it while he has the power to stop it. However, to admit that God is responsible for sin is not necessarily a statement about his moral involvement in it. The judge is responsible for committing a man to prison, but we do not

intend to imply any moral guilt on the part of the judge. In
the same way God is not morally responsible for the
suffering that follows the Fall. None of his direct
punishments upon Adam and Eve were morally wrong;
the violence and evil in the world today are the invention
of man. The fact that the criminal committed to prison
refuses to be reformed by his punishment and spends his
time planning and perfecting the very crimes that sent him
to prison does not reflect moral guilt upon the judge who
put him there. Even if the judge, with some special insight,
knew the man would remain unreformed, he would still
not be morally guilty for the outcome of a just sentence.

Responsibility is not necessarily a statement about
morality. Before we accuse God of some immoral act in
allowing sin and suffering we must remember the
alternative. It is within the power of many governments to
limit their present crime rate by a massive reduction of
personal liberty. It may be true that there are syndicated
crimes, sinister cults and open immorality in a free
democracy that are almost unknown in a totalitarian
regime. Without defending for one moment these evils,
we may defend the system of free democracy that, by its
tolerance of the individual right to think and its respect
for personal convictions, gives rise to excesses and abuses.
In other words, a belief in the value of the individual must
hold even when the individual abuses his rights. The
alternative is to subject conscience, thought, personality
and all freedom to the repressive regime of the
government's will; all dissident thinking will be ruthlessly
crushed. Many nations today have chosen to accept some
violence and evil in their society as the necessary price of
freedom and respect for the individual. They consider the
alternative to be a greater and unacceptable evil because it

violates basic human rights. Perhaps mugging could be virtually eliminated by the stern enforcement of a national curfew from 6.00 p.m. But we do not hold the government morally responsible for the present muggings because they have not ordered such a curfew. We consider our personal liberty to go out or to stay at home worth the violence that this very liberty encourages in some. Surely it is like this in God allowing man to fall into sin, with all the consequent suffering of the present world. The alternative would have been for God to establish an oppressive regime that dealt with man as a robot. Besides, as we have already noted, God *has* done something very positive about man's sin and, as we shall see, the state of the world is not entirely without meaning. You cannot believe in the value of freedom and complain against God for allowing man a free choice that he promptly abused.

4.
Sense out of suffering

Saturday, 26 May 1973 was one of those sweltering late spring days when the sun rules in a cloudless sky; it was just right for a wedding. As the two hundred friends arrived at the parish church the bridegroom was already in his place, smartly dressed in a new blue suit and his shoes brilliantly reflecting the brightness of the day. In traditional but subdued conversation the congregation discussed and guessed at the bride's outfit. When she arrived she wore an attractive lilac dress, made of crimplene with long sleeves and a short skirt; her hair was decorated with flowers. The young bridesmaids completed the scene in their neat blue dresses with floral yokes. The day and setting were perfect and everyone was excited and happy. It would have been like any other wedding, except for the fact that both the bride and the groom were confined to wheelchairs.

Between them, Graham and Tessa had spent a total of sixty years either in hospital or residential care. These two wartime babies suffered from an infantile paralysis that left them with little or no muscular use in their legs and with Tessa's speech so seriously affected that it took her many years to learn to articulate normal sounds. Life, for both of them, had been a long and consistent struggle. They fought against loneliness, the indifference of society ('At one time mother could have buried me in the garden',

...ays Tessa, 'and no one would have known'), the
...rustration of the disabled and then the over-
...rotectiveness of well-intentioned institutions that could
...ot imagine the possibility of Graham and Tessa living
...ormal lives. Graham courted Tessa on the promenade at
...Vestcliffe when he manoeuvred his chair close to hers. To
...old hands meant instant immobility for both of them!
...hey were engaged for ten years, more out of wishful
...ptimism than practical hope. It was impossible for them
...o live a normal married life and Tessa would never
...nanage to run a home; besides no one built married
...uarters for wheelchairs. 'People just didn't realize that
...ve've got feelings just as much as anyone else,' Tessa
...eflected, 'and I really wanted a home of my own. I
...vanted to be doing something; I didn't want to be a
...abbage.'

Today when I visit the home of Graham and Tessa they
...nswer the door first by an intercom and then by an
...utomatic latch-opener. Beyond that, the home is like any
...ther. The doors are a little wider than normal and a few
...tems and work benches are set at a low level. But Tessa is
...nistress of her own home and Graham is responsible for
...etting up the Teasmaid for the morning 'cuppa'!
...Washing, cooking and most of the housework are shared
...by Graham and Tessa, and every Tuesday morning they
...wheel off to the local supermarket to buy the weekly
...groceries. Tapestry and rug-making occupy Graham, and
...knitting and dressmaking keep Tessa's free time well
...filled. Each week horse-riding and swimming complete a
...busy programme; holidays abroad are all part of their art
...of living. Do they never get annoyed or frustrated? 'Yes
...often,' admits Graham, 'especially when I'm trying to put
...my shoes on and tie them. Sometimes I get fed up and just

leave them undone!' And Tessa? 'Yes, when people let m
down, fail to turn up and disarrange my day.' Graham
and Tessa are always ready to laugh and share the
enjoyment of life, and they rarely miss their place i
church on Sunday.

They have known doubt. Shortly after their marriag
circumstances were very hard and for the first time Tess
questioned, 'If there's a God, why has he done all this t
us?' Graham had no answer. They battled through th
dark days of doubt and came into the light of seeing a wis
purpose behind even their disability. I asked Graham wh
God should let them be handicapped. (They claim tha
they don't 'suffer' and will not let me use the word!) Ther
was a pause while he slowly and with great effort ease
himself upright into his chair: 'We've been put here as a
example,' he responded, a little short of breath, 'to show
what can be achieved through four wheels instead of two
legs. God could have healed us; but he didn't want to
because he wanted to show people what could be done
from a wheelchair, and that one could cope.'

If Graham and Tessa have proved anything, it is tha
life is bigger than physical health. I know you don't have
to be a Christian to learn this, but in their case it is a firm
belief in a God that has given them a sense of purpose and
fulfilment in life. When Graham tells you that his purpose
in life is 'living and working to the glory of God' it is no
empty cliché; he has learnt it in the school of frustrating
disablement. Graham and Tessa believe that it is people
who are without God who are really handicapped; they
readily admit that if you took God out of their life the
world would contract so much that they would have
nothing left.

Why me?

The first question that springs to the lips of most people when confronted with an incurable disease, disablement or tragic bereavement is often: 'Why should this happen to me?' It is a natural question and generally requires a soft and gentle answer. However, I want to cast gentleness aside and go straight to the nub of the answer: 'Why not?' That may sound hard and unfeeling, but have you ever stopped to ask yourself what the question, 'Why me?' really means? It is mostly an expression of ignorance, conceit or selfishness!

If you are an atheist and therefore refuse to allow the existence of a personal and sovereign God, then you ought to know better than even to ask the question. It is simply blind chance that brings suffering (or at best the uncontrollable foolishness of other people) and since chance is by definition unreasonable it is only a very ignorant person who will ask it questions. 'Why me?' presupposes some rational cause of events, some orderly being who is responsible for what happens in my life. I cannot escape the conclusion that a belief in no God and a thorough-going materialistic view of the universe is the most meaningless, and therefore the most depressing, world-view possible. Is there absolutely no more to be said when floods devastate my home than that 'A depression in the Bay of Biscay deepened a little and extended a marked trough of low pressure with convergent airs across northern France towards the Low Countries. An old front became revitalized and swung round the northern part of the circulation to affect south-east England'? On a more serious note, can I only describe a terminal illness or a horrible deformity or a heart-

breaking tragedy in terms of the malformation of molecular structure? The response that shrugs complacently and mutters about 'That's the way things are' is an insult to rational and spiritual man who finds himself crying spontaneously, 'Why?' I suggest the atheist should never ask this question either on behalf of himself or anyone else, unless, of course, he is happy to settle for a scientific answer based upon meteorology or medicine. If he does ask such a question for any other reason, then he has at once compromised his atheism. 'Why me?' is an exclusively spiritual question that implies an ordered and wise purpose behind the events of the world — events that happen not by chance. I concede that it is in some ways easier to be an atheist because you don't have to think or ask questions, but for the same reason it is harder to be an atheist because there is no possibility of making sense out of suffering. Admittedly, the atheist may *use* suffering in a similar way to the Christian (bringing out the best in us and so on), but he does so in the knowledge that he is the helpless victim of blind and irrational chance that strikes without ultimate reason or purpose.

However, 'Why me?' may be asked by a questioner, who believes in God, in a way that is nothing more than conceit. The question assumes that although I may not be perfect, I am really not such a bad person and it is wholly unfair for God to pick on me. I imply that my life is sufficiently good to justify a clear run, free from all pain and suffering. This is sheer conceit. No one who believes in God should dare to be so impertinent as to conclude that a man or woman deserves anything. We have all broken the greatest commandment, which, according to Christ, is that we should love God with all our heart, soul and mind (Matthew 22:37). Why should I escape the

effects of sin? Why should everyone else hear the warning voice of God through suffering, and not me? I cannot surely expect to enjoy the good that comes from life and be fenced off against the problems that everyone else faces. To think myself above suffering assumes that I am virtually God himself or at best that my perfect life places me on a par with the angels in heaven! When I think like this I have forgotten how holy God is and how holy his standard of rightness is.

I fear that 'Why me?' frequently has a selfish ring about it. We would never verbalize it quite like this but what we sometimes mean is 'Why me, and not someone else?' It only needs stating in this way to be condemned. None of us would like to admit to being guilty of willing our suffering upon someone else; but I am afraid that is how it often comes across: 'Look at all the wicked in the world. Why me?' Or we may speak on behalf of a friend or colleague who has been hit suddenly by unexpected suffering: 'He's such a kind and good man; never did anyone any harm. Why did it have to be him?' The firm implication is that somewhere there is another man walking about who would be a much better candidate for the suffering. When people think like that I can only be very grateful that the *ultimate* control of suffering is not in the hands of men. Sooner or later they would come round to seeing me as prime candidate and, 'Why me?'!

You may be thinking, 'Doesn't the question simply ask for a reason for the suffering, so that it can all be turned into good use?' I wish it did, but very few people who say, 'Why me?' have such a noble end in view! It is better to be honest than pious and I think all too often we are ignorant, conceited or selfish. If we *really* want a reason, so that we can step into God's plan for us, then the

question is wrongly worded. 'Why me?' usually lays the stress upon *me* and that is the give-away; we are chiefly concerned for number one and not the purposes of God. If we are serious about wanting a reason we should be asking, 'What purpose, Lord?' and not 'Why me?' No one should say, 'Why me?' and only the Christian can sensibly ask, 'For what purpose?'

Part of our fabric

The story of Graham and Tessa could be multiplied without end, and there are many cases far more tragic and heart-rending than this. But the principles of their lives can stand for everyone. In our first chapter we considered the causes and reasons behind both man-made and 'natural' disasters, but disease and deformity seem to be a world away from disaster. They are so uncontrollable and inevitable and while many of us will mercifully escape tornadoes and volcanoes none of us is free from the ravages of disease and, sooner or later, death. We have already seen in our second chapter that before Adam sinned there was no disease, pain or death; and if man had not sinned, deformity would have been unknown. In the third chapter we discussed the fact that a natural bias to sin is passed on from each generation to the next; the theological term is 'original sin'. By this God shows us how inevitably our lives affect our children; there is a spiritual heredity as well as a physical one. But I want to add something further here. The entry and continuance of disease and deformity in the human race demonstrates that there is an inseparable relationship between the spiritual and the physical, the soul and the body, morality

and health.

Disease came into the experience of mankind only because mankind sinned. But it is not simply a punishment, for then some would constantly ask the question framed by the disciples when they passed a blind beggar on the road: 'Rabbi, who sinned, this man or his parents, that he was born blind?' (John 9:2.) Jesus' reply, 'Neither this man nor his parents sinned,' did not mean that they were without any personal sin in their lives, but that the blindness was not due to particular sins on the part of the family. In other words, the blindness was the result of the fact that all men are sinners. Just as the most God-fearing and clean-living man must die, so all men must suffer. It is part of the fabric of our fallen nature. Sin has warped man's entire existence. But, as we have just remarked, disease and disablement are not simply punishments for particular sins (though some diseases may be, and syphilis is an obvious example); disease, like disasters, is a warning. It warns us that disobedience to God spoils the whole of man's life. Many people assume that they can sin with impunity; they can live without reference to God, and it makes no difference. After all, you cannot see a soul, and in this hard-nosed materialistic age men think they can live as they please without any evident response from God. But disease and deformity are a powerful way in which God shows that it is not as simple as that; men carry around in their bodies the evidence that sin reaps a tragic harvest. In 1887 Friedrich Nietzsche spoke of the 'senselessness of suffering'. I am not surprised. Nietzsche was only being consistent with his philosophy of Nihilism that affirmed God to be dangerous imagination, all existence to be meaningless and all moral values to be empty nothing. He became a

victim to his own views and in 1900 died as a result of overwork and — loneliness! Nietzsche was completely wrong in claiming suffering to be senseless. Pain makes men think and forces us to ask questions. Only a fool refuses to learn lessons even from the hardest parts of life.

Suffering shatters

The doctor tried to head off my next point before I got to it: 'I know you talk about the blessings of suffering, but quite frankly that is not my experience. I have seen more people shattered and ruined by suffering than helped by it.' Somerset Maugham wrote in the same vein that suffering does not ennoble character, but makes it petty and vindictive. I'm afraid there is too much truth in this. The story of Graham and Tessa is the exception and not the rule. For every person who triumphs over disease and pain and deformity, there are many who become bitter and hard and who withdraw into a cocoon of fear or misery. If, however, we will not listen to what God is saying through the sufferings of life, then who is to blame for the hopeless despair that results? Given that man is sinful, is he generally better or worse for the fact of disease and pain? First-class health and strength are no guarantee for making a man take stock of his life. If this world of disobedience to God was free from all disease and pain, nothing would make men take life seriously. Pain makes men think. In the New Testament Paul wrote of a time when he experienced such severe suffering in his life that he felt it was 'the sentence of death'; but he knew there was a purpose behind it: 'This happened that we might not rely on ourselves but on God' (2 Corinthians 1:9). Later

on, he explained that the purpose of a particular 'thorn in the flesh' was 'to keep me from becoming conceited' (12:7). Now that is the problem of men today. We are conceited. We think we are quite capable of managing our lives without reference to God. Man is the master of his own fate and captain of his own soul. We can cope very well without God. And when man, by using the mind and the world that God has given him, is able to destroy a particular disease, his conceit is increased. The evidence of this lies in the fact that many today still accuse Christians of believing in a God of the gaps. By this they mean that God is a useful 'filler' for the gaps in man's knowledge. If we do not know how a thunderstorm works, we invent a God whom we invest as the God of the thunderstorm. Then as our knowledge increases, so the 'gaps' left for God to fill become less and less. This is man's conceit. He has a strange idea that knowledge nudges God out of the universe. On the contrary, the more we learn about this incredible universe, the more we should appreciate the greatness of the God who made it. Besides, there will always be problems of pain and suffering for which man has no effective solution. He never will find his own answer to the ultimate in suffering — death.

The existence of disease and deformity is therefore partly intended as a constant reminder of the fact that man is *not* master of his own fate. The disablement of Graham and Tessa has made them more sensitive to others and more appreciative of life. It has made them both *think*. Somerset Maugham was not wholly correct: suffering can and does 'ennoble the character'. It may tragically be true that for many 'one cloud is enough to eclipse all the sun,' but the sun is still there. Helen Keller

lost both sight and hearing as an infant of nineteen months and was consequently dumb. She learned to read and lip-feel, and graduated with honours from Radcliffe College, Boston. When she wrote in 1903, 'Although the world is full of suffering, it is full also of the overcoming of it,' Helen Keller was her own evidence of the truth of this. If suffering and disease are an argument against God, what do lives like those of Graham and Tessa and Helen prove? 'Even pain', wrote Amy Lowell in *Sword Blades and Poppy Seeds* (1914), 'pricks to livelier living.' It is no criticism of God if many allow suffering to 'shatter and ruin' them instead of ennobling. Given that man is sinful, he is better off for the existence of disease and pain. At least they act as some kind of check to his wild career and make him think. Remember Meyer's perceptive comment that 'Physical suffering is a smaller calamity than moral deliquency'? And Lewis's that pain is a 'roadblock to Hell'?

Why doesn't he let them die?

There are some conditions of mental and physical abnormality that seem to be so severe that it appears cruel to fight for the life of the patient. Is it better to let the spina bifida baby die? What useful future has the mentally and physically handicapped spastic? Sadly, of course, many infant deformities and adult disabilities are the result of man's own errors or sin. The thalidomide children are an obvious example. In such cases our answer must be to repeat what was said of man-made disasters earlier. We should not be asking why God allows it to happen, but why man is so ignorant, foolish and disobedient that he

causes such tragedies. However, it has to be admitted that these man-made deformities are possibly the smaller proportion of the whole. I am not concerned to debate the issue of euthanasia here; others have done so, and it is not the scope of this book. However, it is becoming an alarmingly popular idea that we can simply 'put down' our problems. A leading social worker was recently discussing the acute dilemma of what should happen to adult mentally handicapped persons when their parents, upon whom they are totally dependent, die. She wrote of an imaginary young man: 'Even if he is secure and well cared for in his family setting, there is too often the gnawing question, "What will happen to him when we die?" Is the answer years maybe in the back wards of a subnormality hospital or, if there is no better alternative, to be permitted to die peacefully at his parents' wish with his security still around him?' I am not unaware of, or unsympathetic to the problem raised here, but the solution, however tentatively offered, is spine-chilling. It is certainly not a Christian solution. The great difference between the medical doctor and the veterinary surgeon is that one fights for the life of his patient whereas the final solution for the patient of the other is to take out a gun and shoot it! When we turn our doctors into vets, we have turned society into a farmyard. The civilized society cares for its less able members: it works for a 'better alternative'. The brutish society simply puts them down.

Perhaps some would have said of baby Graham when, at three months, he had no future beyond a wheelchair, 'It would be kinder to let him die.' Certainly it could have saved money, time and energy on the part of those who cared for him; but we are now back in the farmyard where life is measured simply in fatstock and market prices. The

quality of life, the inspiration and even productivity of
Graham and Tessa have well repaid society for its care.
But no one could have known this when they were babies.
Parents and doctors fight for a life because, handicapped
as the child may be, he has a right to live. Tessa once
declared to me, after a meeting convened to discuss the
issue: 'If abortion on demand had been available when I
was born, I would not be here now.' But only a criminal
would deny Tessa the right to life. She and Graham have
more freedom than many of the world's great sportsmen
or celebrities. This is no less true of the mongol or spastic.
Many live full and happy lives and prove to us all that life
does not depend simply upon mental alertness and
physical mobility. And that is another reason for disease.
Through it man is taught that life is more than health and
strength. When the man with perfect fitness, who is
nevertheless depressed and miserable, observes the life of
Graham and Tessa, he is forced to ask where such joy and
happiness come from. Once again deformity can make the
careless man think. You do not have to be a Christian to
agree with the words of Thomas De Quincey in *Vison of
Life* (1845): 'Either the human being must suffer and
struggle as the price of a more searching vision, or his gaze
must be shallow and without intellectual revelation.'
Graham made a similarly profound observation when he
claimed, 'People who shut God out don't understand the
world.' The world is too full of examples of triumph over
illness and disability, and joy through pain, to brush them
aside as irrelevant. They challenge the healthy to more
sober and thoughtful living and rebuke the
hypochondriac who enjoys the fear of losing his good
health. When the disabled go horse-riding and swimming,
enjoy holidays abroad and fill every moment of life with

positive meaning, the most convinced atheist should stop and think. It is so often true that those who climb Snowdon enjoy the summit far more than those who travel up by rail! Such thinking may not lead a man to God; after all, there are many invalids making no Christian profession who nevertheless live positive lives. At the same time his thinking ought to challenge the materialistic philosophy that man is no more than an intelligent ape at best, or a conglomeration of chemicals at worst.

Dying too soon

It was Children's Day in Thailand, 14 January 1978, and the hospital minibus was returning to Manorom. Eight adults, including some of the senior medical staff at Manorom Hospital, and nine children had spent an enjoyable and carefree morning watching the picturesque bustle as the rice harvest was loaded onto the barges at Phao-Ha. The children had joined excitedly in the task of filling with rice the large baskets that Thai workers carried to the barges. It had been a restful and happy time for the overworked hospital staff and a rare opportunity for the children to spend time with their busy parents. Ian drove carefully along the Central Thailand highway and Noel remarked appreciatively, 'Thanks a lot, Ian, it's been a beautiful morning.' 'We're not home yet,' replied Ian with a smile. Suddenly a heavy lorry pulled out from behind an oncoming bus and smashed head-on into the minibus. Instantly five adults and seven children died; the rest were left injured in the tangled wreckage.

In this appalling and apparently senseless tragedy the

mission hospital was bereft of some of its most experienced personnel, and young widows, widowers and orphans were created in a moment. One young doctor in the hospital operated to save the lives of the injured knowing that his wife and two little girls had died in the crash.

All the adults were Christian missionaries who had dedicated their medical skills to the service of those who were otherwise denied the full benefits of modern medicine. Each of them could have found lucrative appointments in their home country. Ian Gordon-Smith, for example, was a brilliant young surgeon who had held posts in seven British hospitals and was working at the Manorom Christian Hospital on leave of absence from his position of Senior Registrar at St Mary's Hospital, London. His professional colleagues spoke highly of both his character and his valuable contribution to medicine. Professor Dudly at St Mary's wrote in *The Lancet*: 'His death at an early age is a great loss to British surgery.'

Perhaps the issue that raises itself most forcibly in a tragedy like this is not simply the question: 'Why?', but 'Why this waste of life?' The Christian cannot simply hide behind the guilt of the drunken lorry driver, though that is a factor we have dealt with elsewhere. God must be in control, and he could have prevented it. This was not by chance. One small 'coincidence' will illustrate this. Ian wrote to his parents every week during the two and a half years that he and his wife Stephanie worked in Thailand, and not one letter arrived more than a few days late. None, that is, except one. The first post received in England after the accident included an airmail letter, correctly stamped and addressed, that had taken two and a half months to arrive! In this letter Ian described what

happens when a road accident occurs in Thailand and he concluded,'Out here it's always the person in the bigger vehicle who is responsible — always!' God knew all about this accident beforehand and watched a happy party of young families and experienced medical doctors ride into sudden death. Didn't they all die too soon? The oldest was only thirty-seven years and the youngest two years. Why this waste of life?

Let me begin by repeating what I have said before. At least the Christian can ask this question. He can ask the question because he asks it of an intelligent, reasonable and personal God. The unbeliever cannot ask the question at all. He is left without the possibility of making *sense* of it; the most he can do is try to make the *best* of it. Random chance doesn't have reasons, only results. On the other hand, how does the Christian begin to face the challenge of a useful life cut down before its end? That, of course, begs the question. To believe, as the Christian does, in a God who has an ordered purpose in life means that the death of Ian Gordon-Smith and his family and colleagues was not 'before its end' but 'at its end'. It is true that medical staff claimed that Ian had pressed into thirty-seven years what many take twice that time to achieve, but he, and even the children who died, had all contributed to life. Their life, though shorter than that of many, had been purposeful and useful. Premature death is a relative matter. Before what? Before threescore years and ten? But that makes life nothing more than a sum total of years in existence on earth. The Christian has a better way of measuring life than that. Throughout his Christian life Ian had wanted always to put Christ first, before even his family and his medical career. 'Lord, enable me to be consecrated to your service. To put you first in all things.'

Ian recorded these words in his diary six years before his death. And his last entry expressed the desire that he might 'with God's help, achieve something for Him in His time.' God achieved what he had planned through Ian's life, and through the others, including the children who died on that day. For the Christian, life, however short, is always purposeful.

Within weeks of the accident two doctors and an anaesthetist had offered themselves for the work in the Manorom Hospital. In Thailand and around the world lives were challenged by the single-minded Christian purpose of Ian Gordon-Smith and his colleagues. Their influence for good may well prove to have been greater in their death than in their life. The reality of a God who could motivate men and women with such love for the Thai people, and who could take despair out of such an apparent tragedy, was a witness far greater than the sorrow and tears caused by those deaths.

Referring to death in his later years, Sir Walter Scott claimed, 'The long halt will arrive at length and close all.' That is not the Christian view. Death may close this life, but not all. The Christian believes in a life beyond the grave. There is always something more. At one time the coins of Spain were stamped with the two pillars of Hercules representing the great rock of Gibraltar and Mount Ceuta on the Moroccan coast. Above the two pillars were stamped the words *'Ne plus ultra',* 'no more beyond'. Then, late in the fifteenth century, Christopher Columbus sailed across the Atlantic and discovered the Americas. The word *'Ne'* was struck off the coins leaving simply *'plus ultra',* 'more beyond'. *That* is the Christian hope. Those sudden deaths on a Thai highway were by no means the end. The Christian is certain of 'more beyond'

where, through Christ, life reaches a fulfilment unknown
here on earth. I want to come back to this in the last
chapter, but such a firm hope of a life beyond the grave,
where children and adults can be taken beyond pain and
suffering into conscious enjoyment of the reality of
Christ's presence, makes sense out of suffering.

It may seem strange that Christians, who have such a
firm confidence in a future life with God, should defend
the right to live and the value of life here. William
Wilberforce, the outstanding social reformer of the
eighteenth and early nineteenth century, was a deeply
committed evangelical Christian. He lived life to the full
and threw himself into it with untiring zeal. Lord
Macaulay, the brilliant historian of Queen Victoria's
reign, remarked at the death of Wilberforce that this
desire to live he found strange in a man with so firm a
belief in a future world and with 'an impaired fortune, a
weak spine, and a worn-out stomach'! Wilberforce,
however, as every true Christian, believed firmly in the
value of life here as well as the life to come.

Summary

Out of the problem of pain and suffering we have drawn
some positives. We have seen that disease shows man the
inseparable link between the spiritual and the physical. It
is because of sin that disease and disability first entered
man's experience. In this way such suffering becomes a
warning, and it is intended to make man think and take
stock of his life. It makes man ask questions and search
for answers, and if that leads him to discover the reality of
God's answer then the sharp stab of pain has been

worthwhile. We have freely admitted that suffering
shatters and embitters the lives of many, but it is no
criticism of God if a man fails to make proper use of his
disability. That it *can* be used positively is evident from
the life of Graham and Tessa. Suffering also places a
check upon the conceit of man who thinks of himself as
self-made and master of his fate; this is a fatal error! It is
also true that everyone has the right to live and has the
possibility of living a full and satisfying life. Real life, with
meaning and purpose, does not depend upon health and
strength and this is a lesson only the suffering of some can
teach us. The *'plus ultra'* of the Christian hope adds a new
dimension to all suffering, and we shall return to this in
the last chapter.

5.
Offering alternatives

While we are not all good at running our own lives, most of us are adept at giving other people advice and 'solving' their problems. To listen to a lot of people talk, you would think that God himself is in great need of the benefit of their opinions! To be honest, I used to live like that, setting up my opinions as a useful ground plan for the Almighty to work on. But when I came across Isaiah 40:14, I was put back in place: 'Whom did the Lord consult to enlighten him, and who taught him the right way? Who was it that taught him knowledge or showed him the path of understanding?' There are a number of explanations or alternatives that we put up to answer the problem of suffering or to offer a better solution to it.

It all happened by chance

The idea that God began everything is simply a non-starter to the atheist. Somehow he feels himself secure in the notion that since he has no faith to defend, the problems of pain and suffering can never be an embarrassment to him and his faith in unbelief is therefore unassailable. The atheist does not have to square the evil and violence of this world with the morality of a sovereign God who ought to do something

about it. To him, everything happens by chance and death ends all conscious existence; death is the gateway to oblivion. Dr Francis Schaeffer succinctly describes this view of man and life as 'energy shaped by chance'; so it often seems easy for the atheist to ridicule the Christian's faith and throw rocks at his God. I want to toss a few stones back! At a number of points the atheist is hard put to it to give a reasonable answer to some of the issues that arise from his own faith. There are significant problems in being atheist.

We are often told that the basic instinct in all life, including the human race, is that of self-preservation. Good and bad are therefore simply the result of this instinct. Philosopher scientists like Charles Darwin, Herbert Spencer, Leslie Stephen and Thomas Huxley called it Evolutionary Naturalism. Stephen, for example, put it like this: 'Morality is the sum of the preservative instincts of society, and presumably of those which imply a desire for the good of the society itself.' During his Romanes Lecture in 1943 Julian Huxley, a confirmed atheist and grandson of T. H. Huxley, objected to this statement of Stephen as too narrow and added: 'Honesty and truthfulness are further implications of evolutionary ethics, since they are the intellectual lubricants of free and equal co-operation, and the basis for collective knowledge, as well as an expression of respect for one's own and others' individual integrity.' That is a fine, high-sounding explanation of the origin of good and any atheist would be proud of it. Yet Huxley was strangely silent about where bad comes from. Where did dishonesty and lies come from, if honesty and truthfulness are part of the 'intellectual lubricants' for those 'preservative instincts', if we may mix two quotations?

Speaking during the war years, Julian Huxley denounced the Nazi ethics as 'not just different from ours, but wrong and false'. Then, as if aware that he was making an absolute statement when the whole tenor of the lecture was going to be in praise of ethical relativism, he added, 'or at least less right and less true'! But it was too late to turn back and Huxley's lecture is full of absolutes. For example, he speaks of morality as higher and lower degrees of value and the higher degrees are more permanently satisfying and involve 'a greater degree of perfection'. We may ask, 'And what is *perfection* if it is not an absolute?' Similarly, he claims, 'It is clear on evolutionary grounds that the individual is, in a real sense, higher than the state or the social organism.' That is an absolute for Huxley and if you disprove it his whole moral basis falls. But evolution does not necessarily prove any such thing. Nazism certainly would deny it; so does practical Communism today and so do many world religions. Again, Huxley says morality is good if it is 'the most desirable direction of evolution'. Fine, but who judges what the most desirable direction is? Nazism thought it involved the extermination of five million Jews! Besides, even Huxley cannot hold to his absolute consistently. He asks the question: 'Was Gauguin[1] right to leave his wife and family to devote himself to painting?' This is a good test case and Huxley's reply is most illuminating. 'Yes,' he responds to his own question, because of Gauguin's 'genuine and informed sense of vocation'. Where then does this leave the 'intrinsic worth' (as Huxley elsewhere calls the value of the individual) of

1. Paul Gauguin was a nineteenth-century French post-impressionist painter who left his family in order to live in Tahiti and paint.

Gauguin's wife and children? On his own premise, Huxley should see that individuals are 'in a real sense higher' than 'an informed sense of vocation'! For years atheism has been trying to knock down the morality that comes from a belief in God, but its alternatives are unconvincing.

However, I can understand a man believing that the basic instinct in nature is self-preservation, the determination to survive. When you look at today's world you observe that the nation that is unable to defend itself is annexed to the one that can, and the man who stands up for himself treads upon the one who does not. But nobody believes the world began just like it is today. Let us imagine that evolution is correct in its theory of cosmic star-dust dropping into the ocean and turning into a primitive single-celled substance — or something similar! It should be obvious that when the first blob of something crawled out of the mud and eventually became two blobs, the best means of survival was not to kill each other but to team up. Everyone must agree that mankind would survive better if he never fought, and lived in perfect harmony. So how did the spirit of violence get into us in the first place? It is possible to argue that those two blobs of something might well have decided to team up and then the history of the world would have been very different, but unfortunately, faced with the choice of working together or fighting, they took the wrong decision. But this argument only avoids the issue! If self-preservation is one of man's basic instincts, then as soon as it became apparent to the blobs of something that they had made the wrong choice, they should have called a meeting of fellow blobs at which they would agree to live at peace for ever. In fact, on the contrary, most observers today see that the human race has a bent for its own destruction.

Man too often behaves like the poor ignorant lemmings, those little arctic animals that set out to swim vast stretches of water to find more food and better conditions and drown by the thousands in the attempt. The lemmings are not deliberately trying to commit suicide, but that is precisely what they achieve. The mass migration of the lemmings is little more than 'organized insanity', and that is exactly how someone has described the history of man.

The origin of evil is thus a much bigger problem for the atheist than for the Christian. The Christian can account for it and has an answer to it. The atheist loses on both scores. To be consistent with his philosophy the atheist cannot expect any answer to the question: 'Why suffering?' and does not need even to ask the question. 'Chance', the keystone to his philosophy, is neither moral nor rational. Life is without ultimate purpose. The Christian, on the other hand, must have an answer, because he believes all events are not by chance. We must each decide whether purposeless pain is better than purposeful pain, or more accurately whether a philosophy of hopeless agnosticism is better than a philosophy of realistic optimism.

Cutting out the pain

'Thank God for inventing pain'! You will probably wince at that and respond in anger: 'Hold on a minute, that is precisely where God has gone wrong. Why doesn't he cut out the pain?' Anyone who has nursed a relative in agony has felt the heartache of helplessness. A body contorting with the sharp spasm as if a serrated knife had been

plunged deep and twisted; a face grey and lined and wet with the body's exertion to control the suffering; a little child clenching its fists into a white-tight grip and screaming with bewildered agony. If I was God, I would certainly never let this sort of thing happen. I would cut out the pain with one master stroke of omnipotent surgery.

Imagine a world without pain. A baby lies peacefully in its pram on a warm day in August, soaking in the sunshine and breathing the fresh clean air. A passing insect lands and takes a drink of infantile blood, others join it. A wasp stings, flies bite, and soon the little face is covered in blood and swellings. Maggots are laid in the sores. But the baby sleeps on. Nothing hurts. There is no cry, no alarm to trouble a careful mother. A child experiments with stolen matches and scorches a large chunk of flesh from its leg. But a sock soon hides it and it is days before mother observes the gaping wound oozing pus. No pain; no alarm. The engineer never feels the chain sink into his back, the hiker is unaware of the adder's bite and the fireman has no sensation of heat as he fights the blaze. No pain; no alarm. Pain is God's protective system to man. It warns him of a bad tooth, a broken bone or a hidden growth. Pain says something is wrong and it gives man the opportunity to put things right.

Does pain, however, have to be so severe? Why cannot God cut it out at a certain threshold? Surely you can see the answer to this. Generally the more intense and prolonged the pain, the more severe is the problem causing the pain. If pain shut off at a certain threshold, how could we be sure that we will not simply ignore the problem once the warning had stopped? My alarm is set for 6.00 a.m. each morning, but it rarely goes off. I have

developed a habit of waking between 5.45 and 5.59 each day! I simply reach out and cancel the alarm. Sometimes I then ignore what it would have told me if only I had left it alone! None of us would endure pain voluntarily. We would all switch it off if we could, and that would be disastrous. One of the continuing battles safety officers wage in modern industry is against the worker who removes the safety guard, carries out his task and then carefully replaces the guard!

'Thank God for inventing pain.' It was Dr Paul Brand who said that, and he had spent three years with a team of researchers trying to invent an artificial pain system for limbs that had lost their feeling. He abandoned the task when he realized the impossibility of matching God's complex system. What makes Hansen's disease (leprosy) so frighteningly disfiguring is just that it is painless. Limbs are without feeling and can be burned, cut, scalded or simply worn away without the patient knowing. Only pain avoids disfigurement. Given the fact of a world in which disease and accidents are possible, pain is a friend. I know it does not appear this way in the agony of a terminal illness, but we were glad enough of its help when we trod on a nail, grabbed a hot poker, ran a splinter in our hand or blinked at the grit that flew into our eye. Next time you wake up at night with excruciating cramp, thank God for that pain; without it your leg might have been black by morning!

Looking after his own

There often appears something contradictory about a Christian suffering. If it is true that Christians are 'a

people belonging to God' (1 Peter 2:9) then why does God
not look after his own? 'He can't be much of a God', says
someone, 'if he doesn't even take care of those who trust
him.' When floods come Christians drown, in a fire
Christians burn and in a famine Christians starve. Surely
God can do better than that! Before we answer this
challenge and give a reason for the suffering of Christians
let's be clear about one thing. If God did look after his
own in a such a way that every Christian was always kept
free from tragedy and suffering, you can be sure the
challenge would simply be rephrased: 'Ah', men would
sneer, 'those Christians only trust God because he keeps
them out of trouble; they have taken out a spiritual
insurance policy that offers good dividends annually and
matures handsomely at death.' It's a 'Catch-22' situation
again, isn't it?

In the early days of missionary work men talked of 'rice
Christians', those who professed to have become
Christians simply because the missionaries gave 'rice' to
the Christians. As a matter of fact, this is precisely the
challenge Satan threw against God when he wanted to
question the sincerity of Job: 'Does Job fear God for
nothing? Have you not put a hedge around him and his
household and everything he has? You have blessed the
work of his hands, so that his flocks and herds are spread
throughout the land. But stretch out your hand and strike
everything he has, and he will surely curse you to your
face' (Job 1:9–11). So there is nothing new in the
challenge; it has been used for centuries. But it is strange
to hear people say, when they see a wealthy Christian for
whom life appears comfortable and easy, 'Of course he
believes in God, it pays him to, doesn't it?' and then, when
they observe a Christian in great pain and suffering, 'Why

doesn't God do something about it, if he loves him?'

In fact, the book of Job is all about this very question. Glibly people say Job is all about suffering. That is not quite accurate. The great debate in the book of Job concerns itself with this issue: 'Can a man love God not just for what he gets out of it?' Satan said man cannot and that if God took everything away from Job he would 'curse you to your face'. God said man can, and he would prove it through Job. God won his case. Job lost everything — his property, wealth, family, friends and health — but he refused to deny his faith even when his wife said to him, 'Are you still holding on to your integrity? Curse God and die!' (2:9.) This is one reason why God often allows Christians to suffer just like everyone else. In this way he can show a critical world that men and women can love him because of who he is, and not just for what they get out of it. God is as much against 'rice Christians' as his strongest critics are. Christ was scathing towards those who followed him around merely because he had fed five thousand men with a handful of bread and fish: 'You are looking for me, not because you saw miraculous signs but because you ate the loaves and had your fill' (John 6:26).

Christianity is not about how to escape from the difficulties of life, but about how to face them. The Christian belief in heaven is not an escape from *now,* but a hope for *then.* By allowing Christians to suffer, God shows that he can make people of sufficient moral and spiritual calibre to face the events of life and to face them with joy and certainty. Soldiers are not trained in five-star hotels but in rough barracks and on barren hillsides; God doesn't want an army of softies, but a legion of men and women strong enough to face life as it is. Paul wrote to

Timothy, 'Endure hardship with us like a good soldier of Christ Jesus' (2 Timothy 2:3) and that is precisely what every Christian should expect because in that way he can prove the value of his faith to the issues of life. Through suffering God teaches his people patience and humility and keeps them from becoming proud or self-confident. On the other hand, there are countless occasions when God *does* protect his people in a special way.

It was April 1942, and the crippled troop-ship *Llangibby Castle* pushed her erratic way across the Bay of Biscay. She was two days out from Gibraltar and heading for the coast of England. Accompanying her was a lone destroyer, H.M.S. *Whitehall*, an old 1918 'V. & W' Class, easily outgunned by the German Narvic destroyers that prowled off the French coast at that time in the war. The weather was unusually perfect for the bay. The sun shone down from an unclouded sky, a light north, north-east breeze barely troubled the blue waters of the Atlantic and carried a spring-like weather off the coast of Portugal. Visibility was uncomfortably good for the labouring troop-ship and her escort. Able Seaman Blaker stood in the crow's-nest, high above Vera Lynn singing brightly from the mess radio, and sang to himself as he swept his glasses across the far distant horizon. Blaker was the only professing Christian on board the *Whitehall*. Just before midday on the second day out from Gibraltar, the wind banked to the south-west and a shallow, narrow patch appeared in the distance. 'Smoke dead ahead, sir', Blaker tried to identify it. A ship on fire? A patrolling Narvic? The *Whitehall* steamed bravely into the unknown. The 'smoke' proved to be a cold, damp mist that unexpectedly enveloped the escort and her charge and reduced visibility to a few yards. Soon after entering the mist, the crews

listened to the irregular beat of two or three Focke-Wulf four-engined reconnaissance planes as they searched for convoys. A few minutes later a second flight droned above the two vulnerable ships and disappeared into the history of war. As suddenly as they had entered the mist, H.M.S. *Whitehall* and the *Llangibby Castle,* affectionately nicknamed 'Elsie' by Captain Bayer and his crew, broke out into the remainder of this perfect spring day with all its promise of summer. Commander Russell closed his men to action stations. If the masts of the two ships had stood out above that strange and unaccountable mist then they could expect a force of destroyers to move in or a pack of hungry U-boats to gather for the kill.

The crew of the *Whitehall* hurried to their posts and waited, tense and determined. The troop-ship ploughed on astern. Nothing happened, no one came, and the two ships steamed northwards under clear skies and an unruffled sea to the safety of an English port.

Whatever you may think of this story, I can vouch for its truth in every part and there was no natural explanation for such an isolated and timely patch of mist. A man may bluster about 'coincidence' or 'imagination'; he may simply dismiss it, like the crew did, as 'so-and-so lucky', but it all sounds a bit more authentic than that, doesn't it? Given my belief in a personal God, there can be little doubt that here he was at 'action stations' for a lone believer on board. I cannot escape the conclusion either that a complement of more than two hundred and fifty men benefited from God's care for one Christian. Such accounts can be multiplied without end. I have chosen this one simply because I have authentic knowledge of it. The history of the Christian church and the narratives of the Bible itself abound with examples of God's

intervention on behalf of his people. In his later teaching career that crow's-nest look-out used his experience to illustrate to generations of young people the reality of God's protection of his people as they escaped from Egypt (you can read the story in Exodus 14). But God makes no unconditional promises, preferring that Christians should trust in his wisdom rather than in a guarantee of immunity.

Give them all a chance

Some people live in areas of the world where famine and floods are part of life. Others have never even heard the gospel of God's love in Christ. These people seem to be a long way behind in the race simply because others have a head start. Why doesn't God give them all an equal chance? Why doesn't he make sure *everyone* hears about Christ, if it is so important? And if there must be floods and famines, why don't they come in equal proportions everywhere? Doesn't the Bible itself say that 'God treats everyone the same'? But it certainly doesn't look like it.

In the first place it is not true that God treats everyone the same and the Bible never claims this. Certainly this is how the *Living Bible* paraphrases Romans 2:11, but the words are more accurately translated in the New International Version: 'God does not show favouritism,' and in the context the issue is whether the Jew has more claim upon God than the Gentile. Paul's argument is that on the subject of salvation all men are equal. If a man rejects the truth (v.8) he can expect only 'wrath and anger', whoever he may be. God is not impressed by a man's colour, race or religion; Christ, and Christ alone, is

the way of salvation. So, according to the Christian faith, *all* men will stand before God on the Day of Judgement and only *one* test will apply: 'What do you think of Christ?' In that sense there is no favouritism with God.

The fact that many people live in deprived areas is largely due to the results of man's sin and we discussed that in an earlier chapter. The appalling suffering and loss of life in a flood that occurs in Bangladesh is always far worse than the same kind of flood on the west coast of North America and the reason has nothing to do with unfairness on the part of God. It is all to do with the poverty, flimsy homes and generally poor sanitation and communications in one country, and the solid buildings and efficient state relief in the other. The same argument is true of those who live in deprived areas of our own country. Their lack of opportunity in life is tragic, but if selfish greed did not govern the lives of so many of us such deprivation could easily be eliminated.

The question remains, why doesn't God ensure that at least everyone hears the gospel of Christ if, as the Christian claims, it is so important? Then at least they would seem to have the same chance of eternal welfare, even if by man's fault they cannot enjoy equal welfare here. The fact is that wherever man lives, and in whatever conditions he lives, he is sinful by nature and by practice. 'All have sinned and fall short of the glory of God' says the Bible (Romans 3:23) and no man, whoever he is, *deserves* anything from God. That is the first thing we must understand. But secondly God *has* in fact revealed himself in a way that every man ought to be able to understand. Listen to Paul again, in Romans 1:19–20: 'What may be known about God is plain to them, because God has made it plain to them. For since the creation of

the world God's invisible qualities — his eternal power
and divine nature — have been clearly seen, being
understood from what has been made, so that men are
without any excuse.' In other words, the whole of natural
creation tells man that there is a God and that he should
be worshipped. Every man has this witness wherever he
lives. He has no excuse for not believing in God. If in the
face of all this man ignores his conscience and chooses to
reject God or to exchange the glory of the immortal God
for images made to look like mortal man and birds and
animals and reptiles (v.23), then man has only himself to
blame for the consequences.

You may counter, 'That's all very well, but where the
gospel of Christ *is* taught surely the view of God and
salvation is so much clearer?' I am glad you think so! But
the promise of Christ to those who 'ask, seek and knock'
(Matthew 7:7) is not confined to those who have actually
heard of Christ. God will find a way to bring the true
gospel of Christ to anyone who sincerely searches for the
truth and prays for a knowledge of the true God.
Evidence of this fact is found in the New Testament in the
life of the Ethiopian (Acts 8), Cornelius (Acts 10) and
Lydia (Acts 16). Each of these had sought the true God
out of a pagan background and their path led them first to
Judaism before God met with them in the gospel. God's
activity in creation, in history and in the conscience of
man is what Paul referred to when preaching to the
Athenians in Acts 17: '. . . so that men would seek him and
perhaps reach out for him and find him, though he is not
far from each one of us. For in him we live and move and
have our being' (vv.27,28). The experience of the
Ethiopian, Cornelius and Lydia is not confined to Bible
times.

I want to relate an account that illustrates how God can meet up with a man who is searching for an answer to life, but who has never heard of Christ. I personally know David and have met and talked with Kaka; I can assure you of the truth of the whole episode and I have added nothing to it.

Kaka's childhood was set in the isolated mountains of Nepal where he grew up knowing only the rigorous life of a semi-nomadic shepherd. In 1943, at the age of eighteen, he began to grow restless and dissatisfied with the hard life of the mountains. At this stage his quest was undefined and vague. He was looking for a big something — some kind of answer to life, an answer to his longings. He expected to find it somehow in religion or in ascetics, or in God, or perhaps in a combination of all three. Kaka heard that there was a war on, and rumours reached him that the British in India were recruiting strong young men from the mountains to fight in their special Gurkha regiments. This was his golden opportunity and he left his father's sheep in the care of a friend and ran away from home. Kaka joined the British Gurkha army and began his training as a soldier. In 1946, he went to Japan with the British occupation forces, and there he served ten months as a full-dress guard at the emperor's palace. After Japan, most of his military service was restricted to hot spots in India, fighting against the Chinese in a number of border disputes both in Assam and in northern Kashmir. All those years, as part of an agreement Nepal had with recruiting governments, he and his companions were carefully shielded from any exposure to Christianity.

After twenty-two years of military service, Kaka returned to his own home village as a retired soldier. At that time, to collect their yearly pensions, retired soldiers

had to travel out of the mountains to Gorakhpur in northern India. The full journey took anywhere from three weeks to a month for men like Kaka who lived in isolated parts of the country. Once inside India, the last leg of the journey was completed by train. In January 1967, on his second such journey, Kaka and his companions were travelling on an Indian train when a white woman approached them and asked in Nepali, 'Are you Gurkhas?' to which they replied, 'Yes, we are.' The woman then offered them three small booklets written in Nepali for the price of one rupee. Kaka bought a set and the woman quietly disappeared. Without realizing it, Kaka had purchased a Gospel of John and a collection of Scripture verses.

Later, in his leisure, when Kaka had a chance to read the booklets, he experienced a strange sensation. 'Surely these really are the words of God,' he thought. He read to his companions and they agreed that these were no ordinary books. But the more he read, the more puzzled he became. He couldn't make out what the message was, and what he was to do about it. Above all, he couldn't make out who this one called 'Jesus Christ' was. Strange things were said about him. One of the booklets said, 'Believe on the Lord Jesus Christ and you shall be saved.' 'How do I believe on him?' he thought. 'I don't even know who he is. And what does it mean to be saved? Problems too deep for me! Better ask the religious experts.'

When he returned home, he called together some of the religious men, a strange collection of shamans, seers and one or two with a rudimentary knowledge of Hinduism. 'What do you make of it?' he asked. The shamans merely shook their heads and the Hindus, after some discussion, concluded that 'Christ' must be the same as 'Krishna'. But

Kaka wasn't satisfied. The books kept haunting him. He began to carry them with him everywhere he went. In his spare moments, watching his cattle on a hillside, he would read from the booklets. He read till they were tattered and torn. He longed that someone would come and explain their hidden meanings to him. Once or twice he even asked travelling Tibetan lamas about it, but they, like the rest, could give no answer.

Almost three years later, in October of 1969, Dave Watters and a companion stood on a high, lonely pass in north-west Nepal, lost in a blizzard. They had been travelling for three weeks through a wild and unfamiliar territory, trying to learn something of the size and whereabouts of a tribe Dave wanted to speak to about the gospel of Christ, and also to determine the best place to settle among them. And now the way ahead seemed utterly impossible. From the top of the pass there was nothing before them but a complicated maze of cliffs, each one sweeping off hundreds of feet below. Hardly knowing what to do, the travellers suddenly realized to their amazement that a strange set of footprints had forged on ahead. They decided to follow them. On they went, working from one cliff to the next, sometimes across narrow ledges, sometimes across rock slides, but always following the tracks. The snow was no longer falling, but dry snow on the ground was blown about furiously by the wind and the two missionaries considered it incredible that the tracks remained clear and uncovered.

After hours of negotiating through breath-taking terrain, the tracks suddenly brought Dave and his companion onto a small but well-travelled mountain trail. Night had already fallen and, totally exhausted, they

slept right there on the trail. Early the next morning they followed the trail for another two hours until they came to a small mountain village. On inquiry about other travellers, they were told that no one had come over the pass for several weeks. The villagers insisted that the missionaries were the first travellers since the snows! From that day on those footprints on the snow were called 'angel tracks'.

Dave Watters was now on the fringe of the tribal territory and he decided to settle there. The area was remote, wild and very cold and it seemed ridiculous to bring a wife and two small boys to such a place. However, the 'angel tracks' rekindled his courage with the assurance that God had gone ahead. Dave was reminded of God's word to the Israelites: 'See, I am sending an angel ahead of you to guard you along the way and to bring you to the place I have prepared' (Exodus 23:20). He returned to Kathmandu for his family.

A few months later Dave and his family were settled in a village just across the river from Kaka. They had never met, but Dave decided to search in Kaka's village for a steady, reliable man to help him with the language. As he approached the village he came across a half-dozen men standing at the village entrance chatting. Suddenly his attention was caught by one of the men and a strong conviction swept over Dave: 'That's the man. You take him!' He went straight to the man and said in Nepali, 'Do you think there might be someone in this village who could come with me to Kathmandu and help me learn your language?'

'If you looked around, I suppose you might find someone,' the villager responded indifferently.

'I'm not looking any further,' Dave replied. 'You're the

man I want!'

'Well, then,' Kaka said, 'we'd better go to my house and talk it over.'

There Dave met Kaka's wife and family and, after settling on a few practical matters, he agreed to go with Dave on the following day. That night, however, after going to bed, Kaka began to have misgivings. 'Why did I agree to go?' he thought. 'How can I get out of it now?' After a night of tossing and turning, he finally fell asleep and had a dream. He dreamed that he saw Dave and his wife Nancy come to his village. The missionary walked up to Kaka and said, 'You come with me,' and he picked up his rucksack and followed them down the trail. When Kaka woke up he knew from his dream that, regardless of the outcome, he must follow.

The next day when Dave went to see if Kaka was ready, the ex-Gurkha warrior was prepared for the long journey, but hesitated for a moment. 'Before we go I want to ask you a question.' He took from a little metal box three tattered booklets and declared, 'These books tell of one called Jesus Christ. Do you know anything about him?' Stunned by the remarkable providence of God, Dave answered, 'Yes, I do.'

'Well then,' Kaka responded firmly, 'I'll go with you if you promise me you'll explain these books to me, and teach me everything you know about Jesus!'

That was the beginning of a deep and lasting friendship and Kaka soon became a devoted follower of Christ. Today he is in charge of a growing, vigorous church, steering them with courage and wisdom through times of persecution and ministering to them in a beautiful and unselfish way. Without knowing where to look, Kaka had been asking, seeking and knocking, and God had

answered.

God also comes to some who reject his overtures of grace. In his autobiography *The Other Half: A self-portrait* Lord Kenneth Clarke, who would consider himself a liberal secular humanist, describes a religious experience he once had: 'It took place in the Church of San Lorenzo, but did not seem to be connected with the harmonious beauty of the architecture. I can only say that for a few minutes my whole being was irradiated by a kind of heavenly joy, far more intense than anything I had known before. This state of mind lasted for several minutes, and, wonderful though it was, posed an awkward problem in terms of action. My life was far from blameless: I would have to reform. My family would think I was going mad, and perhaps after all, it was a delusion for I was in every way unworthy of receiving such a flood of grace. Gradually the effect wore off and I made no effort to retain it. I think I was right. I was too deeply embedded in the world to change course. But that I had "felt the finger of God" I am quite sure and, although the memory of this experience has faded, it still helps me to understand the joys of the saints.' The writer to the Hebrews has something to say about just such an experience in Hebrews 6:4–6.

Ultimately, as Jonah learnt during his submarine experience, 'Salvation comes from the Lord' (Jonah 2:9). God provides for it, initiates it and applies it to a man's life, giving him faith to believe. However, we have seen enough to realize that there is nothing fickle and arbitary in this. There will never be a man who truly searches for God with all his heart who will not find him, and we have a promise from God himself for this: ' "You will seek me and find me when you seek me with all your heart. I will be

found by you," declares the Lord' (Jeremiah 29:13,14).

Getting rid of the big ones

Almost always when people suggest that God ought to put a stop to violence and evil in the world, they are thinking about the violence and evil committed by other people. This is not really surprising because few of us have a wish for our own destruction. So it is other people's sins that God ought to do something about, not mine. After all, 'they' are the ones who cause all the misery. Why can't God see this? If he got rid of 'them', the big sinners, the world would be a much better place! How can he stand back and watch men of great evil and violence get away with making so many people unhappy?

Just for a moment let us suppose God thought this to be an excellent idea and a simple remedy for the evils of the world. So, at a stroke, he removes the men of outstanding violence and cruelty. The mass murderers, the sadistic torturers, all the cruel and violent men have gone; for a while we breathe freely. Then we begin to notice that men whom we considered not such great sinners by comparison are now the worst. So we demand that God should deal with them because they are spoiling the world. So, at a stroke, God removes the men who beat their wife and children, and those who steal great sums of money violently and those who pervert justice. Without them the world looks much better, for a while. Then the lesser criminals, the shoplifter and the brawling drunkard, the small-time burglar and the mugger become the biggest sinners in the world and they are spoiling perfect happiness. So, to keep in line with our request

God removes them all at a stroke. For a while, we really think heaven has come — until we notice the man who dodges his fare on the railway, and the neighbour who gossips about us down the road, and the postman who kicks my dog over the fence for barking at him. Our anger rises and, quite rightly, God removes these biggest sinners who are spoiling happiness. At this point I am a little uncomfortable because I have a suspicion that some of my friends have noticed my 'little' sins which now seem enormous because all the big sinners have gone. In line with strict justice I find God has placed me next on the list because, though I never thought it possible, *I* am spoiling the world and stopping it from being perfect. *I* am contributing to the unhappiness, although I always thought it was the 'big sinners' alone who did this.

When I was a student I worked vacations for a fruit farmer. One year he decided, for a change, to grow some ducks and the day came when I was asked to select the biggest ducks for market! That was easy. I jumped in among the unsuspecting creatures and bundled the biggest half-dozen into a crate. The problem was that as I now looked at the ducks that were left some of them appeared nice and plump. Just right, I thought, for market. Certainly they were bigger than all the others. So out they came and into the crate. But when I looked back at the duck pen there were still some bigger than the rest. They were not as big as the biggest ones in the crate, but they were much bigger than the smaller ones in the pen! However many I took out, there were always some left that were big by comparison with the rest in the pen. I had the same problem grading beans and apples.

When you expect God to remove all the big sinners in the world, remember that very soon that means *you*. Now

one day this is exactly what God is going to do. Speaking of heaven, he says, 'Nothing impure will ever enter it, nor will anyone who does what is shameful or deceitful, but only those whose names are written in the Lamb's book of life' (Revelation 21:27). The rest are excluded from heaven. That is what hell is all about. Then why does he not do that right now and finish with all sin? Because God has left a little while for men to turn to God. He is patient with our sin, not wishing that any should perish but that all should come to repentance. So, as Paul put it in Romans 2:4, 'Do you show contempt for the riches of his kindness, tolerance and patience, not realizing that God's kindness leads you towards repentance?' Perhaps it is just for *your* sake that God does not remove all the people who spoil the world!

There was once a farmer who chose best quality seed when he was planting a field of wheat; the seed was good, the soil was good and the farm workers did their job well. Unfortunately a neighbour had taken a dislike to him and during one night he scattered weeds among the corn. Of course, no one knew until the spring, and as the young shoots broke through the ground so the weeds appeared. 'Sir,' said the farm workers, 'do you want us to go and pull them up?' The farmer decided against this. 'Because', he replied, 'while you are pulling up the weeds, you may root up the wheat with them. Let both grow together until the harvest. At that time I will tell the harvesters: "First collect the weeds and tie them in bundles to be burned, then gather the wheat and bring it into my barn."' Christ told this story in Matthew 13 and he was touching upon our very problem. God lets the evil and the righteous live alongside each other for many reasons, and one is this: to root out all the bad people would often adversely affect

the good people. The world as we know it would simply grind to a halt if everyone who rebelled against God was taken out of it. The surgeon who is keeping a Christian alive, the marketing manager who is keeping a Christian in business, the lawyer fighting the just cause of a Christian and the social worker striving to find a job and accommodation for an unemployed, homeless believer — Christians need them all in this life. When Christ brings this world to an end he will then 'weed out of his kingdom everything that causes sin and all who do evil' (Matthew 13:41). But he does not do this now, for the sake of the Christians. Besides, there is something that Christ's story of the wheat and the weeds could not easily illustrate. In real life, every day, some of the weeds are turning into wheat! It is a good thing, therefore, that God did not pull up all the weeds at once.

6.
Why doesn't God do something?

'Just look at the mess!' Why doesn't God do something about it?' I am always pleased when someone puts the problem to me like this because it is the perfect cue for a positive Christian response. Right at the beginning of this book we made it clear that the Christian response to suffering is not negative and defensive, but positive and hopeful. Living in the same world as you do, I am confronted with the same appalling tragedies and am aware of the cruel behaviour of many men towards their fellows. I have faced the issues and given some reasons and responses. But one reason why I am a convinced Christian is that on this particular issue I can offer a faith in a God who has some very positive and practical answers to the state of today's world. My God is not passive. He has taken action and there are no solutions offered by men to this problem that are so effective or so 'tried and tested' as those designed by God. And he does not offer them as desperate remedies for an uncontrollable tragedy. He planned these remedies even before sin and its consequences came into the world. I have five positive answers to the question: 'Why doesn't God do something about it?' There is no special order in these five. Together they make up the Christian response and any one is incomplete without the others.

The Maker's instructions

One of those container lorries that look rather like an office block on ten wheels had parked in the side street. The bewildered driver crossed the road and approached me with a delivery note in his hand. He stubbed his finger at the top of the sheet and asked in despair: 'Can you tell me where this place is, chief?' I knew it well; I had visited in that road many times. But right now my mind went blank! Certain that everyone he had already asked would have been 'just visiting the area', 'lost myself, mate', or 'not speak English', I was anxious not to fail him. I hastily marshalled my thoughts, gave the directions and warned him of the difficulty of squeezing his juggernaut into the small suburban streets ahead. As his vehicle pulled into the maze of roads, I suddenly realized that when I said, 'Third on the right', I really meant 'Third on the left'! If we ever meet again, I only hope that driver does not recognize me!

Inadequate instructions from God to man would be bound to cause road-blocks in man's history, but in fact the tailback of sin and suffering in the world stems from man's first collision with the Maker's instructions. Earlier in this book we saw how man fell into sin and fell out with God. But God did not wind up the world like a gigantic clockwork toy, spin it into space and then stand back until it wound down or fell apart. Repeatedly God has interfered in man's history to give him instruction, guidelines on living. Most people in a society with some kind of Christian roots are aware of the Ten Commandments and the Sermon on the Mount; not many people know them, but they at least know they exist. The Ten Commandments were given through

Moses, and you find them in Exodus 20. They begin like this: 'God spoke all these words' (Exodus 20:1). The Sermon on the Mount is the teaching of Christ nearly fifteen hundred years later and you find it in Matthew 5 to 7. In fact the whole of the Bible is God teaching man. Whatever people think today, the Bible is the most relevant book we possess. It may not have too much to say about the science of heart transplants, cancer research, nuclear physics or black holes in space, but these issues as pure science, however important, have little bearing upon human relationships. Science is neither moral nor immoral, it is amoral. In some quarters to be a nuclear scientist is almost a criminal offence. This is nonsense! Radiation that, misused, can kill and maim thousands can also be harnessed for the reduction of cancer cells. Microscopic lenses that can invade the privacy of a home may also search for disease in a patient's stomach or diagnose a defect in a developing foetus. It is the *use* of such sciences which affects man's history and well-being — and that is precisely where the Bible comes in. What science has never been able to do, God does permanently in his Word. He gives clear instructions governing man's relationship with man. The Bible is God's word to man in every generation and culture. It is the surveyor's ground-plan, the architect's drawing, the engineer's blue-print to guide man through life. In the Old Testament David made this claim for the Bible: 'Your word is a lamp to my feet and a light for my path' (Psalm 119:105), and Agur claimed, 'Every word of God is flawless' (Proverbs 30:5). Paul, in the New Testament, made the same point this way: 'All Scripture is God-breathed and is useful for teaching, rebuking, correcting and training in righteousness' (2 Timothy 3:16). It is simplistic but

perfectly true to say that if man followed the Maker's instruction life on earth would be a whole lot better. A main part of the reason for the appalling suffering in the world today is that with the advent of modern science man thought he had dispensed with the need for God. Having thus transferred his allegiance from the Creator to the scientist, man lost his guide-line, which alone could control his *use* of radiation and pin-head cameras. Our biggest problem today is not the relentless progress of science, but the remorseless degeneration of morality; morality must have an absolute authority.

During the last war a United States Air Force bomber was returning to base at Benghazi after a bombing mission over Italy. The plane disappeared and it was assumed to have run out of fuel and crashed into the sea. Seventeen years later an oil exploration crew found the bomber 420 miles south of Benghazi in the middle of the Libyan desert. All the flying and navigational instruments were in perfect order. On that fatal night during the war, the automatic direction finder needle had informed the aircrew just when they passed over their base, but owing to a strong tail wind the bomber had arrived over the base much sooner than the crew had anticipated and they concluded the instruments were faulty. They flew on into the desert until, running out of fuel, the bomber crashed into the sand. Eight men died in the blistering heat of the Libyan desert because they distrusted the indications of the instruments. When we foolishly ignore God's instructions, the Bible has its own comment to make: 'There is a way that seems right to a man, but in the end it leads to death' (Proverbs 14:12).

You may respond, 'Wait a minute, it's governments and the political, religious and philosophical systems that

make the world such a place of misery and suffering.
What has the Bible to say to governments — never mind
the individual?' I suggest you are asking the wrong
question, based upon a false premise. The Bible says very
little to governments, but it says a great deal to people —
and what are governments, if they are not made up of
people? Most of the 'freedom fighters' and political
agitators today, in fact, everyone who opposes a
'government', are simply trying to change a system. If
they succeed, they generally substitute another system
with all the blemishes of the first, plus a few more. The
Bible sets out to influence *people*. If you try to short-
circuit the biblical approach you will ultimately fail
because, even if your political philosophy is a good one, it
will never work better than the people who operate it, and
they can only work properly if they have a morality
controlled by the Maker's instructions. You could hardly
find a greater contrast between the philosophy of the
Tzars and that of Stalin, but whose Russia was better
from a humanitarian point of view? The disagreement
among historians in answering that question proves the
point. It is not so much the system as the people operating
the system who cause the suffering.

So, the first way in which God has 'done something' is
through the Bible, a reliable account of God's plan and
purpose for mankind. The airline pilot may choose to
ignore the fire bell sounding in his ears and the red light
flashing on his instrument panel, warning him that his
B.A.C.111 has an engine on fire; he can still attempt to
take off. But who will be to blame when the aircraft
plunges to earth with a horrifying death toll? The
manufacturer or the pilot?

A new start

Terry had drifted through life with a huge chip on his shoulder, believing that the world owed him a living. He was sleeping rough when we first met him, but after a few months he was fitting into a normal family life, holding down a job and the future looked hopeful. Sadly he drifted back, ran foul of the law, and ended up years later as an alcoholic with his health shattered and his world falling apart. We talked together and, looking at this 'old' man in his mid-thirties, who could have been so active and useful, I found myself saying in all sincerity: 'I'm sorry Terry, we tried hard to help, but we failed.' Terry looked up and smiled at my naivity. '*You* failed?' he queried, and then shaking his head sadly went on, 'No, *I* failed, the trouble lies in me.' Terry was right and he had made an admission that few are willing to make. The problem of the world lies in the heart of man, which the Bible says is 'deceitful above all things and beyond cure. Who can understand it?' (Jeremiah 17:9.)

Although God has given us his Word, so that we are without excuse, he has not left us there. God offers man a new start and a change of heart. Paul described this in 2 Corinthians 5:17: 'If anyone is in Christ, he is a new creation; the old has gone, the new has come!' Christ himself expressed it plainly when he told Nicodemus, a religious leader of the day, 'You must be born again' (John 3:7). This 'new birth' is the second major way in which God has 'done something'. Becoming a Christian is not simply a matter of knowing the rules or even just trying to live by them. Anyone who sets out to obey the Bible will soon realize what a high standard it is, and unfortunately it is not long before we find ourselves

kicking against it. We are spiritually 'dead' in sin (Ephesians 2:1) and 'hostile' towards God (Romans 8:7) and those two facts account very largely for the man-made misery in today's world. What religion or philosophy offers a new birth and can keep the promise? Only Christianity! When you become a Christian God has put his Holy Spirit in your life, and since the Holy Spirit is the third Person in the Godhead, this is the same as saying that God himself takes up residence in the life of the Christian. Peter says that this means a man can 'participate in the divine nature and escape the corruption in the world caused by evil desires' (2 Peter 1:4). You see, our bias to sin can only effectively be overcome when we experience the new birth. 'If anyone loves me' Christ claimed, 'he will obey my teaching. My Father will love him, and we will come to him and make our home with him' (John 14:23). What Christ is saying here is that obedience to his Word is only possible when God comes into a man's life. That is the new birth. This is what Terry needs. He doesn't need just rules and regulations; other religions can supply those even if they are not up to the standard of the Bible. He needs a new start, a new birth. This new birth changes the way a man thinks, feels and acts and goes a long way to restore the proper image of God in man which, as we saw in chapter 2, Satan has vandalized and defaced.

We always blame everyone in general for spoiling the world and many blame God in particular; but as Terry so honestly admitted, '*I* failed, the trouble lies in me.' Do you remember the section called 'Getting rid of the big ones' in the previous chapter, and the illustration of the ducks? Surely you cannot deny that the best way you can help alleviate the evil in today's world is to start with

number one. When God gives *me* a heart of love, a spirit
of peace, a mind of purity, a will gladly submissive to his
Word and a soul in harmony with the Creator, then this
must overflow to those around me. That is what Jesus
meant when he said that Christians are 'salt' and 'light'
(Matthew 5:13,14). The real Christian, the one who is
born again by God's Holy Spirit, brings the flavour of
God to an unsavoury world and the light of his Word to a
generation in darkness. If that isn't God 'doing
something', then what is?

But how can you be born again and have the new start?
A teenage girl, we will call her Andrea, came to me at the
close of an evening service and said she wanted to become
a real Christian. She had always thought she was a
Christian; she now knew she was not, and could I help
her, please? I talked with Andrea about the way to
become a Christian. She wanted so desperately to believe,
but somewhere there was a block. It all seemed too simple
and straightforward to believe. If I had told Andrea to do
something, she would have done it; if I had given her a
prayer to pray, she would have prayed it. In fact, I sent her
home and told her to sort it out with God alone. The
following Sunday Andrea was back in church and asked
to see me. At once I could see the change. She said to me,
'I became a Christian last Monday.' 'I'm delighted to hear
that,' I replied, 'but why not last Sunday?' This was
Andrea's reply: 'Last Sunday night I was trying so hard to
believe, and I just couldn't. On Monday evening I said to
God, "Please help me to believe," and suddenly I did!'
The Bible says faith is a gift from God just like the new
birth, the new start itself. Christianity is not all about
working up faith, or trying to make yourself believe what
you know is not true. Nor is it a matter of turning over a

new moral leaf and following a new moral code. Christianity is trusting Christ and receiving a new birth by the Holy Spirit; every new Christian is made by God. That is all about God 'doing something' in today's world.

The place of the cross

Some people think of the cross of Christ as the greatest example of the very thing we are discussing in this book: the uselessness of suffering and violence and the apparent indifference of God. It was a tragic end to a good life. The cross is central to the Christian and he has no message without it, but there is no other act in history that has been so misunderstood. And it is not that the instructions are not clear. It is simply that people often do not like what the Bible says about the cross.

In the first place, the cross was no accident or 'last ditch' stand by God to do something to remedy an impossible situation. Listen to these words of Peter in the New Testament: 'He (Christ) was chosen before the creation of the world, but was revealed in these last times for your sake' (1 Peter 1:20). That means God planned the cross as the remedy for sin even *before* man sinned.

But why the cross? Again the Bible has a clear answer, and again we go to Peter: 'He himself bore our sins in his body on the tree, so that we might die to sins and live for righteousness; by his wounds you have been healed' (1 Peter 2:24). Paul has the same thing to say to the Christians in Galatia: 'Who [Christ] gave himself for our sins to rescue us from the present evil age' (Galatians 1:4). So Christ's death was for our sin. We have seen many times already that God cannot just wink at sin as if it

doesn't matter. Sin *does* matter. It is what spoils the world
and makes for misery. *You* think it matters or else you
would not be asking the question that gave rise to this
book. God also knows that sin matters. It is the great
mountain between man and God. When Christ died, he
took that mountain of sin upon himself and suffered
God's punishment in my place: 'God made him who had
no sin to be sin for us, so that in him we might become the
righteousness of God' (2 Corinthians 5:21). God's way to
forgive, and therefore to remove the mountain of sin in a
man's life, is to let Christ settle the account as a substitute
for us. When we ask Christ to do that for us personally
then we are reconciled to God, the road-blocks are
removed, and we can start living as God wants us to. That
will make for happiness all round. Listen to Peter once
more: 'Christ died for sins once for all, the righteous for
the unrighteous, to bring you to God' (1 Peter 3:18). Read
this paragraph again. It is perhaps the most important of
the whole book. Isn't this God doing something about the
problems of the world?

If you are thinking fast you will be ready with your next
question! It will be something like this: 'O.K., but if God
has forgiven the sin of those who trust Christ, and if
Christ has taken their punishment instead of them, why
do Christians still sin and still suffer?' We answered this
point in chapter 5 under the heading 'Looking after his
own', but there is a new twist to the question here. Why do
Christians still sin? The reason is because God has just
started a work in them here that he will fully complete
only in heaven. God does not turn men into puppets when
he turns them into Christians, and the Christian is not yet
perfect. God wants to show the world that Christians,
with all their weakness, can still love and serve God in

today's world.

What we never see

It never seems very helpful when someone says, 'Well, I can't actually prove it to you, but I know it's true,' yet that is the very argument I am going to use here! Of course, lack of solid, scientific proof does not invalidate the truth of a thing. After all, if I relate to you a dream I had last night, how can I ever *prove* to anyone that it actually happened that way? When you ask, 'Why doesn't God do something to restrain the evil and suffering in today's world?' I am obliged to reply, 'He does; he restrains a vast amount of evil that would otherwise be there. I can't show you where he has done this, because if it was there to show you then it would be obvious that he hasn't restrained it!'

There is a clue to what I am talking about in Romans 3:25–26 where Paul writes of the justice and forbearance of God and says, 'He had left the sins committed beforehand unpunished.' In other words, God does not punish all our sin at once and as we deserve. It was Christ himself who said of God, 'He causes his sun to rise on the evil and the good, and sends rain on the righteous and the unrighteous' (Matthew 5:45). God allows enough suffering to remind man of his foolishness in abandoning his Creator, but not too much to cause the world to sink beneath its own weight of evil. When people whimper about the inevitable war that will blast human life and this earth into oblivion, the Christian can assert with confidence that it is God who will end this world, not man. God has the ultimate say. If that is so, then it is obvious that God is restraining excessive sin and suffering

all the time. How many more Stalins, Hitlers and Amins would there have been in history if God had not exercised a restraint upon man? No one can answer this question now, but the Christian believes that in eternity, when the answer *is* known, he will have good cause to thank his Creator for what the psalmist meant when he claimed, 'Your footprints were not seen' (Psalm 77:19). In the previous chapter we spoke of God looking after his own. If sometimes we can *see* how he does this, how often are his protection and care *unseen*?

A family I once knew of owned a boat. They went out to sea one day and a storm blew up, drove them off course and practically wrecked them. It was little short of a miracle that they were saved. When eventually they reached safety and home they boasted of their experience and, without a thought of God, excitedly described their triumph over the elements. But perhaps it *was* a miracle; perhaps they were supposed to observe those unseen footprints of God and in foolishly ignoring the restraining hand of God they wasted God's kindness to them. Now, had they all drowned, someone would have complained about the useless waste of life or the indifference of 'the Almighty'. Since they did not drown, God presumably had nothing to do with the issue! When we are determined not to believe, it is easy to settle for the 'Heads I win, tails God loses' approach to life. But it isn't very honest, is it?

Duncan Campbell who, until his death in 1972, was an effective preacher in the highlands and islands of Scotland, told the following incident of his experiences in the Great War trenches. In a particular battle he was in charge of a platoon and, knowing the odds were against platoon sergeants at this time, he was asked by five other sergeants to pray with them and explain the way of

salvation. All five professed to trust Christ. Only two of the five returned from the battle and Duncan Campbell sent a message to them to join him in prayer to thank God for deliverance. The messenger found them celebrating with the rum rations and they sent back this curt reply: 'Tell Campbell and his prayer meeting to go to hell!' This kind of story can sadly be multiplied without limit, and it may have jolted the memory of a similar experience in your own life. God *is* active in his world. He *is* doing something all the time, and without his restraining power the world would be far worse than it is. How many 'near-misses' are really the intervention of God? How many more Aberfans would there be, but for God? If he lets everyone share in his obvious kindness, like the sun and the rain, then he doubtless lets everyone benefit from his unseen footprints also. These interventions of God, however, are not arbitrary and fickle decisions, like a little boy setting free some of the ants he has collected and drowning the rest in a pond. God always has a purpose for everything, or else he ceases to be God. What then is the purpose of his unseen hand restraining the suffering of the world? Is it not to make the world a little better than it would be if left wholly to man, and to give men time to think, and reason to be grateful? 'Do you show contempt for the riches of his kindness, tolerance and patience, not realizing that God's kindness leads you towards repentance?' (Romans 2:4.)

The ultimate hope

Lillie had spent her life looking after ageing parents. A virtual prisoner to the home, she quietly and lovingly

tended to their needs as the years of opportunity slipped away. She never married and had lived what most would consider a dull and colourless life. Eventually she was left alone and almost at once a severe stroke took away her own health. When I met her she was bedridden, speechless and in frequent severe pain. But of all the people I have known, there are few who could teach me so much, so simply. Lillie died some years ago, but whenever I think of her I have a mental picture of a frail wisp of an old lady propped up against her pillows, and with a wrinkled face wreathed in a smile and her left hand clasped over a painful chest, she is slowly lifting up her right hand and pointing with a finger towards heaven. For Lillie, with little enough to encourage her in this life, her confidence lay in the certainty of heaven. That was her ultimate hope.

In the final analysis there is nothing that settles the question of suffering and sin so effectively as the Christian belief in heaven. A man may ridicule this and dismiss it contemptuously as 'pie in the sky when we die'; but he has nothing to put in its place. Let me wheel in a Graham and Tessa, (chapter 4) and take you to visit a bedridden old lady, and ask you to explain your own philosophy. It must fit the case. The apostle Paul knew what suffering was. He had been shipwrecked, beaten, imprisoned, stoned, ridiculed and all the time he lived with such a frail constitution that at least once he despaired of life itself. But writing to the Christians at Rome he could declare triumphantly: 'I consider that our present sufferings are not worth comparing with the glory that will be revealed in us' (Romans 8:18). Listen also to him writing to the Christians at Corinth: 'Our light and momentary troubles are achieving for us an eternal glory that far outweighs them all. So we fix our eyes not on what is seen, but on

what is unseen. For what is seen is temporary, but what is unseen is eternal' (2 Corinthians 4:17–18). The philosophy that man will fall into oblivion, snuffed out like a candle, makes no sense of the inequalities of life. It provides no hope for the man who is denied everything in this life, and it offers no justice to the evil tyrant who lives in luxury and dies in peace. 'Ah!' says the critic, 'Does the Christian find it so difficult to face reality that he wants some comforting refuge in the thought that God will "square it all" and "get even" in heaven?' This is a parody of the Christian hope. The real Christian is a Christian realist and realism includes the belief that death does not end all. It is no criticism of Christianity that it offers something more beyond the grave; that is precisely where it gains an advantage over the emptiness of unbelief. Faced with the alternative of oblivion and a conscious intelligent future full of activity and life, I have no doubt at all which gives most dignity to man and offers him the greatest hope and meaning through the events of this life. Without such hope the philosophy that Somerset Maugham put into the mouth of poor Dick Stroeve in *The Moon and Sixpence* is all that remains: 'The world is hard and cruel. We are here, none knows why, and we go none knows whither.'

God has certainly done something about the suffering of mankind. He has created a heaven where, according to his own estimate, 'Nothing impure will ever enter it, nor will anyone who does what is shameful or deceitful' (Revelation 21:27). For those who do enter: 'Never again will they hunger; never again will they thirst. The sun will not beat upon them, nor any scorching heat.' 'He will wipe every tear from their eyes. There will be no more death or mourning or crying or pain, for the old order of

things has passed away' (Revelation 7:16; 21:4). The 'ultimate hope' of the Christian is that for those who trust in Christ there is a place where all sin will be absent, where suffering of every kind will be unknown and where joy and peace will be unspoilt. The Maker's instructions, the new birth, the cross of Christ and the restraining hand of God are all leading towards the goal that finally God will be honoured and worshipped in a place called heaven where all suffering is gone for ever. Every man has the right to deny this 'ultimate hope' of the Christian, but if he does, he ought never again to accuse the Christian of believing in a God who has done nothing about the suffering of the world.

It won't go away

I am not so simple as to believe that everyone who reads this book will be convinced by my reply to the question of suffering. But before you go away from this book let me remind you that the problem won't go away and if you reject the Christian answer you must find a better one. That was the challenge I issued right at the beginning of the book. You must have an alternative that stands scrutiny and offers hope and not blind despair. You must find a solution that meets a few basic requirements.

You must make sure that your alternative to the Christian answer is realistic. Suppose I wheeled Graham into your room and said, 'I want you to make sense out of life for Graham.' What would you say? A hearty slap on the back and a breezy 'Cheer up old chap, it's never as bad as it seems,' would be cold and callous. An old Yiddish proverb says, 'If you are bitter at heart, sugar in the

mouth will not help you.' So you will try to be more realistic, won't you? But what *will* you say? If you have rejected the Christian hope, what is left? If you hesitated for a moment, Graham would have filled the silence with his own experience of the satisfying answer of the Christian faith.

You will make sure also that your alternative answer is simple, won't you? A young man came to his pastor for a reference to join the Samaritans. He used to attend church regularly but he never made a commitment to Christ and he embarked on a course of evening classes in philosophy. Courteously he explained that he used to believe what the pastor believed, but now he had grown beyond the simplicity of all this and he expected that one day the pastor would catch up! The minister put a little test to him. He said, 'Steve, you are called out one night to a man standing on the parapet of Kingston Bridge. Life has treated him badly and he can see no purpose in going on. He is about to jump and he cries in despair, "Is there an answer?" Steve, you've three minutes. What will you say to him?' 'Oh,' replied the young friend, 'I would need at least two hours to explain my philosophy.' 'But', the minister persisted, 'you only have three minutes, so what will you do?' Steve smiled and conceded, 'I suppose I would send him to you!'

Well, have you a better answer than that of the Christian? One that makes more sense, faces all the facts and offers a more hopeful future? After all, anyone can destroy another man's house, but he cannot necessarily build a better one.

Finally!

There was a man who ran a well-ordered home where everything was available for the benefit and true happiness of his family. One day the younger son came to his father and said, 'Dad, I find your home boring, and I don't like the restrictions. I've seen and heard about much better things outside and I want to go my own way, live my own life and do my own thing. Just give me some money to start myself off, and you'll see if I can't make a real go of life without you.' Now, the father knew precisely what the outcome would be but, strange to say, he gave his son the money he asked for and sadly watched him leave home to go his own way. Occasionally it looked as though the young man might make it work, but soon the money was wasted and his life was ruined. Everything was spoiled. Even the best pleasures turned sour on him and he was soon reduced to eating pigs' food. He tried everything the world around could offer, but there was great famine in his heart and no one could give him anything to satisfy it. His world had collapsed.

Some people thought the father stupid for giving such a wayward son his freedom; others accused him of cruelty since he knew what the outcome would be. But the father waited patiently. Eventually the young son came to his senses and returned home. 'I've had enough,' he admitted, 'I can't make it on my own; I only mess up my life. I'm sorry; please take me back.' So he placed himself once more under the protection and restrictions of his father's home and there he found his true happiness.

All those years the father had watched and listened in sorrow as his son went deeper into misery. All those years the father was ready to receive his son back. The father's

love allowed the son to go his own way, and the father's love stood back and watched his son eating pigs' food in misery. But the father's love conquered rebellion and restored a ruined life (Luke 15:11–24).

Other books by

BRIAN EDWARDS

Published by Evangelical Press

GOD'S OUTLAW

THE STORY OF WILLIAM TYNDALE AND THE ENGLISH BIBLE

When William Tyndale set out to provide the first printed New Testament in English he was forced to do so in defiance of almost every person in authority. Compelled to flee from his homeland he continued his work of translating the Scriptures whilst slipping from city to city in an attempt to avoid the agents which were sent from England to arrest him. His story is one of poverty, danger and ceaseless labour.

" . . . *a stirring historical narrative , it is full of many spiritual gems which enlighten and strengthen the reader."*

Grace Magazine

"This very interesting and well researched book is written in a popular style and deserves to be widely known."

Elim Evangel

"God's Outlaw is about Bible smuggling - into Britain! . . . Brian Edwards' new biography of Tyndale certainly opened my eyes to the human beings involved in the Reformation. So if you're beginning to take your multitude of versions for granted, read this book."

Buzz Magazine

THROUGH MANY DANGERS

THE STORY OF JOHN NEWTON

An exciting and compelling story of one of the great heroes of the Christian faith. A common sailor at the age of eleven and press-ganged into a man-of-war at nineteen, John Newton experienced the thrill of action, the cruel lash of navy disipline for desertion, and the loose and blasphemous life of a free thinker. This story of the author of *Amazing Grace* will warm every Christian heart and intrigue those who normally have little time for religion.

"The author has . . . given us a book to instruct the mind, edify the soul, thrill the heart. You can give it to your children to read, to your neighbours, to your work colleagues - to anyone . . . In short - this is a brilliant book."
Evangelical Times

"The appeal of this amazing testimony to Christians of all ages and callings will ensure a wide circulation for this excellent book, and through it the grace and glory of God will shine more clearly to every reader."
Dedication

"Gripping to read, it is informative, challenging and calculated to be a blessing to the soul."
Grace Magazine

NOTHING BUT THE TRUTH

AN EXPLANATION OF THE INSPIRATION AND AUTHORITY OF THE BIBLE

Faced with claims that modern science and scholarship have disproved the Bible, many Christians find themselves confused about the authority and reliability of Scripture. Is the Bible really trustworthy, or does it contain errors? This book sets out to answer this and similar questions in a clear and straightforward manner which assumes no previous knowledge of the subjects concerned.

"Written with the 'ordinary Christian' in mind, it attempts to bring the true evangelical doctrine of Scripture within reach of every believer. It is comprehensive in its scope, but not excessively long. Behind the popular approach one can discern painstaking study and careful evaluation of evidence."
Evangelical Times

"Brian Edwards has great ability in being able to write simply on complex subjects; but more than this he grips the mind with the seriousness of the issues involved and carries the reader along with an easy flow of words."
Fellowship Magazine